#MakeUrPenLOUD
How To Be A
Lifestyle Blogger

Inked by: LoudPen
Edited by: LoudPen

Cover Photo by: Megan Weaver
Cover Design by: The InkSpot

Created by: The InkSpot
Published by: The InkSpot

TO MY DEAREST PENNIES AND PENS

This one is for you. You know who you are.

#MakeUrPenLOUD: How To Be A Lifestyle Blogger

Table of Contents

4

Chapter 1: My Story

Dear Pennies & Pens,

It's ya girl LoudPen here to share with you #MakeUrPenLOUD: How To Be A Lifestyle Blogger. Throughout this book, I will be offering advice on how to write about fashion, beauty, music, film, art, travel, and events. Before we get to the meat and potatoes, let me tell you my story.

My childhood was just like The Cosby Show. My parents are both college educated, independent thinkers who love art, music, fashion, cars, business, finance, sports, travel, reading, film, etc. As you can see, they have diverse interests so of course their interests spilled over to my siblings and me.

Growing up, my parents encouraged us to think for ourselves and be explorers. We were only allowed one hour of TV time a day and during summer breaks, my dad would make us read one book a week then write a report that we had to present to him. During our teen years, we had curfews and were limited on the amount of time we could use the phone.

Despite all the rules, our house was truly a fun place to grow up. With two brothers and a sister (plus their friends), I always had someone to play with, spy on, irritate, talk to, etc. We were all pretty popular so we had a ton of friends that were at our house 24/7.

My parents both love to travel so we were always visiting new places. During spring and summer breaks, we went to Hilton Head, the Wisconsin Dells, Maine, Myrtle Beach, Orlando, Phoenix, Gatlinburg, and more. I loved going on vacation with my family and to this day, I adore traveling.

However, what I loved more than anything was reading and writing. I loved books and would read all the time. Books presented a way to escape and dream about a world different from my own. Writing was a creative outlet; a chance to express myself. I always kept a journal and would write about whatever I was going through at the time.

Writing became my secret world because I never shared my writing with anyone. My family knew I loved to write but that was the extent of their knowledge. I never thought my writing was good so I didn't think it was worth sharing.

As I entered my teen years, I started to get more serious about writing or "doing something creative" for a living. Since Jet, Ebony, Essence, Vibe, and The Source were my favorite magazines, I decided I should write for one of them. I thought that writing for a magazine would be exciting and glamorous. Not to mention, I would be able to write for a living.

Upon entering college at the real HU...Hampton University (sorry Howard grads, I had to say that), I decided to major in Print Journalism. I felt that Print Journalism would help prepare me to write for magazines but unfortunately, I was wrong. The program focused on writing for newspapers and for those unfamiliar, newspaper journalism is strictly about delivering the facts in a short and concise way.

While in the program, I was pretty miserable but since I was still young I wasn't taking school seriously. I mean I went to class and got decent grades but I was more concerned about hanging out with my friends than getting an education. Then in my junior year, I was hanging out with one of my friends when I started complaining about hating my major.

My friend suggested that I switch to something I did like because it would make me happy. I immediately shut that down because my parents were paying for my tuition and I didn't want them to have to spend extra money. However, my friend insisted that I should major in something I was passionate about otherwise I wouldn't be motivated to finish school.

Being the fast moving person I am, I immediately went and changed my major to English. I believed that English would be more creative and would teach me how to write. As soon as I became an English major, I did a 360 with school. I started studying more and partying less so my

grades improved significantly. I also started participating in school activities and began writing for The Saracen, my school's literary journal.

I even won first runner up in a writing competition hosted by The Saracen. I didn't go to the awards ceremony because I never thought I would win so I will always regret that. However, it was a turning point in my journey to become a writer because I had finally exposed my writing and was promptly recognized for my talent.

From that point on, I knew writing was not only my passion but my calling. However, I was certain that I did not want to use my real name when publishing my writing. I felt that creating a pseudonym would give me more freedom to express myself and my feelings. I started brainstorming names and decided I wanted something that was completely unique, an original creation concepted for and by me.

I started thinking about words and how people describe me. I'm always being told how loud I talk and I thought that the word "loud" was a great way to describe my writing. Even if it is non-traditional, to me loud writing meant that the writing was so good the words bump on the page as the sound from your stereo does.

The word loud grabs your attention because when you hear loud music, loud noise, or a loud person, you turn around and pay attention. I wanted to make people pay attention, make them listen, to get them to really read and digest my writing.

The word "pen" comes from the fact that I like pens. My mother is a teacher so growing up I would help her grade student's papers and tests. My mom always had a bag of pens so she could grade papers with different colors; I thought this was so cool and it sparked my love for pens. To me, the pen was a masterful tool.

Somehow, I concluded that the words "loud" and "pen" should be combined to create LoudPen. And so, LoudPen was born. A few months after graduating, a friend of mine suggested I start a blog as a way to get my writing out there. I was feeling frustrated because I had no job prospects and no clue what I wanted to do with my life.

After finishing school, I moved back in with my parents because like most Millennials, I was affected by the recession and lack of jobs. However, I knew I couldn't stay there because I didn't want to have to abide by my parents strict rules. I had always dreamed of moving to New York so I figured I should just move. This was my exact thought: "If I don't move now while I have no husband and no kids, I never will."

Once I made my big decision, I set up a few job interviews, bought a one way ticket to NYC, packed 2 weeks' worth of clothes, and found friends to crash with. Somehow through the Lord's mercy, I was able to find an apartment, sustain myself financially, make friends, and have plenty of adventures. I am proud to say that I called New York City home for five years.

My first blog, The Loudest Pen Ever was mostly about 80s/90s Hip-hop and R&B as well as my personal life. I gained a few readers and also created a Twitter account and Facebook page. I maintained the LPE for about two years but I never created a plan or identified what my goal for the site was.

While blogging for the LPE, I was bitten by the fashion bug so I decided to start a blog that was focused on fashion. I created de la Pen in June of 2010 and launched the site in August. I named the blog de la Pen because I thought it was chic and stylish.

The title was inspired by de la Soul (a famous Hip hop group) and Oscar de la Renta (an iconic fashion designer) both of whom I admire. This is why the "d" and "l" are always lowercase. I honestly get mad when people capitalize it because I feel like it ruins the whole effect.

Moving right along, in November of 2009, I attended a WordPress blogging conference called Wordcamp and met my former boss who was looking for interns for her multicultural online magazine. I began interning for her and learned so much about writing, marketing, and creating content for the multicultural consumer.

In September of 2010, I connected with Claire from The Fashion Bomb who gave me great tips on how to attend runway shows and events during New York Fashion Week. With her advice, I was able to cover my first New York Fashion Week. Most of the shows I attended featured the work of emerging multicultural designers.

After attending NYFW, I decided that my site should be an online magazine and not just a blog. I also concluded that it should be international and multicultural. I wanted the site to reach a diverse audience of people from all over the world.

I also wanted the site to feature unique and original content that was extremely high quality. I felt that there was a gap in the market for a high quality magazine for multicultural people. Jet, Ebony, Essence, and Vibe (magazines I grew up reading) were losing relevance because each publication seemed slow and behind. Since these magazines were still printing their latest issues, most of their content would consist of things I had already read online.

This is when it hit me that digital publishing was the way to go. With digital publishing, you could reach more consumers faster than ever. Additionally, you would not have to focus on one area or region because the internet is global.

In October of 2010, exactly one month after covering my first New York Fashion Week, I was invited by The Fund Forum of Arts & Culture Uzbekistan to cover their Style.uz Art Week event. I was shocked when I got the email because I considered myself to be a nobody. I had been blogging for two years covering many different events but I had never been sponsored by a brand.

For those that don't know, Uzbekistan is in Central Asia and was a part of the former Soviet Union. The Fund Forum is a non-profit dedicated to hosting events about Uzbek arts, fashion, and culture. That said they were looking for bloggers and members of the media to come and cover Style.uz which is their art, style, and fashion week.

Somehow, I was lucky enough to get an invite and they sponsored my flight and accommodations. My family and friends told me not to go but, there was no way I was turning down a free international trip. I figured that as long as I prayed about it and hoped for the best, everything would work out fine. I just could not let go of an opportunity like that.

I think my family and friends did support me, but they feared for my safety since Uzbekistan isn't the most popular travel destination. Overall, the trip was absolutely amazing and I am so glad I went! I met famous designers like Domenico Vacca and Igor Chapurin as well as seeing a couture show featuring vintage Dior.

Right after returning from Uzbekistan, I met my amazing business partner and BFF Cacha` Lopez. Cacha` and I met through a mutual friend who thought we would work well together. Cacha` is based in Baltimore so she came to NYC to meet with me, exchange ideas, and discuss a collaboration.

When Cacha` arrived at my apartment, we instantly clicked. I truly believe that it is fate that we met because we are both committed to becoming successful entrepreneurs. As business partners this is such a key trait for us to have because both partners must be devoted to the business. Without dedication, the business will not succeed because the partners will give up at the first sign of trouble.

During my initial meeting with Cacha`, we decided to start a business together. We are both very ambitious so we knew from day one that we couldn't just focus on one thing. We concluded that the company should be called The Network because it was a simple yet classic name. Plus, The Network would allow us to manage multiple businesses under the umbrella of The Network.

At the time, Cacha` had already started her own model management company called Cacha` Management. Meanwhile, I knew I wanted to do marketing and PR so I decided to start a PR & marketing company and

call it Pen PR. A few weeks later, Cacha` and I signed our partnership agreement and so we were officially business partners. The Network was our joint venture that consisted of Cacha` Management and Pen PR.

We decided to work with artists such as models, stylists, designers, musicians, etc. For each client, Cacha` would serve as their Manager and I would be their Publicist. This way each client would have both management and PR. We created a website and signed four models, two stylists, a makeup artist, and two DJs. We represented each artist at different times and we were able to land them a few bookings and a features on blogs.

In mid-2012, we decided to start working with brands and focus on marketing and PR. We landed Latin Fashion Week and The Fund Forum as clients but only for short term projects. We consulted Latin Fashion Week on their New York Fashion Week event and landed sponsors Ouidad and IT Cosmetics. We also booked designers, models, and the venue.

The Fund Forum hired us to create a social media campaign about one of their events, the M&TVA Awards. The M&TVA Awards is a music, TV, and entertainment awards show that recognizes Uzbek musicians, actors, and artists. For the campaign, we focused on creating written and visual content (blog posts, images, and videos) to promote the event.

Cacha` and I had previously worked with a Videographer/Director named Addison Wright so we brought him on to shoot the video for the campaign. Cacha` who is an amazing photographer shot the photos and I handled all the writing. We made a great team even if we did fight and get on each other's nerves on the trip, lol. I should mention that The Fund Forum did sponsor all three of us to attend and cover the event as well as providing a stipend. It was an amazing project and was definitely our first big break as a company.

Upon returning to NYC, we pitched similar projects to other brands but never landed a new client. After a while, we figured that we should put pitching on hold and create our own campaign. Our niche has always been multicultural so we concluded that we should launch a campaign to promote diversity.

Our campaign Flavor NYC was a digital and social media campaign dedicated to promoting diversity in fashion. The campaign focused on a shoot called "New Amerykah" inspired by Erykah Badu's album of the same name. New Amerykah featured 3 multicultural models wearing classic American clothing and accessories. Flavor NYC is definitely one of our most successful campaigns to date and the photos are still on our website.

In early 2013, we decided to build and launch Flavor as a lifestyle brand dedicated to promoting diversity and showcasing the work of multicultural artists. We created a brand strategy and planned how we were going to execute all our ideas. We wanted Flavor to be an extension of our agency because it gives us the opportunity to launch our own creative endeavours and have a brand dedicated to advocating for diversity.

Later that year, I relocated to Houston. I'm not sure when but one day someone I follow on Twitter wrote: "You pay your bills with your 9-5 but you build your fortune with your 5-9." That quote has stuck with me since then. That's when I decided to start developing The InkSpot and writing this book. I finally realized that if I had a profitable business, I would be able to build my fortune.

I told Cacha` my idea about writing a book about blogging and she supported me 100%. In fact, she decided to start a new business as well; Jewels by Cacha` is an online accessories boutique that features simplicity at its best. JBC is dedicated to making modern women look and feel their best at an affordable price.

My company, The InkSpot is an international and multicultural lifestyle publishing, production, and design company. We produce and publish original content to entertain, educate, and inspire our audience. We also design modern, chic products to give our customers the opportunity to express themselves and showcase who they are.

I created The InkSpot because I am going to build my own empire like Jay Z, Oprah, and Tyler Perry. Although, I clearly do not have their money or fame, I have noticed that they each have multi-line businesses. This means they have multiple streams of revenue and can pursue a variety of business endeavours. When I started writing the business plan for The InkSpot, I knew I wanted to do the same thing. The InkSpot is a unique company because while it is a start-up, I am building it with the intention of it becoming a global business.

In December of 2015, I will finally be moving to Dallas and I cannot wait. I truly believe that Dallas is the best place to build The InkSpot and 8515. The city has the nation's largest arts district, a bustling tech and start-up scene, a growing fashion industry, cool music, and delicious food. It has everything I am looking for; business and personal.

When Cacha` and I originally made the decision to pursue JBC and The InkSpot, we also decided to relaunch The Network as 8515. We both still love marketing, PR, styling, and event planning so we did not want to abandon the company. Plus, we knew we would need those services for our new businesses so why not hire ourselves? 8515 provides a platform for us to have in-house marketing, develop our own brands, and have clients.

8515 is a multicultural lifestyle agency and we specialize in multicultural and millennial marketing. We offer marketing, public relations, event production, creative direction, styling, writing, blogging, editing, and social media. We work with fashion, beauty, music, art, travel, and lifestyle brands. We focus on connecting our clients with multicultural consumers through a unique marketing mix to increase engagement and sales.

On April 23, 2015, we will be hosting Flavor's Night Out. Flavor's Night Out is an event created to celebrate diversity by showcasing the work of multicultural artists. Flavor's Night Out seeks to entertain, educate, and inspire attendees.

The inaugural Flavor's Night Out event will feature an introduction of Jewels by Cacha` and preview of JBC accessories presented by Cacha` Lopez, an introduction of The InkSpot and preview of #MakeUrPenLOUD presented by me, and guest speaker Rumal Rackley (son of Gil Scott-Heron) will be speaking about his late father's life and memoir The Last Holiday.

Flavor's Night Out will be sponsored by Middle Sister Wines, de la Soul Sister, Durrah Jewellery, Quinque Inc., Mixtina, and Tipsy Scoop. Flavor's Night Out will take place at Y-Clad's Hidden Gem in NYC.

We are excited about the growth our company is experiencing and we look forward to the future. Please make sure you follow and connect with us online at:

- www.8515agency.com
- www.theinkspotlp.com
- www.allpeneverything.com

As you can see from my story, I have been around the block once or twice. If it wasn't for my happy childhood filled with family, music, film, fashion, art, cars, travel, and love, I never would have developed such diverse interests. My diverse interests led me to starting a blog where I gained writing, marketing, and business experience.

As a lifestyle blogger, I have written about fashion, beauty, music, art, travel, and events. I have met so many different people and learned about a variety of brands. I truly believe that I have mastered the art of creating unique and original content, collaborating with brands, and managing a blog.

With that said, I am ready and willing to share my knowledge with you. #MakeUrPenLOUD is about empowering you to be the best lifestyle blogger you can be by giving you the tools and knowledge to do so. Instead of learning everything on your own via trial and error as I did, I am giving you a guide that will help you become a lifestyle blogger.

Being a Lifestyle Blogger has allowed me to travel the world covering events like New York Fashion Week including The Couture Council Luncheon Honoring Valentino, Artopia in both Dallas and Houston, The Affordable Art Fair NYC, Charleston Fashion Week, Style.uz Art Week, and so much more.

I have interviewed fashion icons like Publicist and Owner of People's Revolution Kelly Cutrone and Andre Leon Talley who is the former Editor at Large of Vogue. Additionally, I have interviewed many artists such as Gene Noble, Marina Romanova-Arnott, Derek Fordjour, Gray Malin, Adam Jones, Vakseen, and more. I have also gone on several press trips, collaborating with brands like The Omni Hotels & Resorts, Lone Star Court, and Hotel ICON.

As far as beauty collaborations, I have worked with Rimmel London, Derma e, Beautisol, Perlier, and St. Ives. Furthermore, I have partnered with fashion brands like Macy's, Durrah Jewellery, and Thirty-One Gifts.

I want to help you create unique and original content for your lifestyle blog because you have to be able to do that if you want to land brand partnerships. Once you build a portfolio, you should start collaborating with brands so you can monetize your blog and/or receive complimentary products and services. In order to do that, you have to know how to pitch to brands so this book covers that as well.

Each chapter of #MakeUrPenLOUD is dedicated to a certain topic such as "How to Conduct Interviews", "How To Plan Fashion and Lifestyle Photoshoots", "How To Attend and Cover Events", "How To Collaborate with Travel & Hospitality Brands", and so much more.

#MakeUrPenLOUD mirrors the diverse content of a lifestyle blog because it covers a variety of topics. I truly believe that #MakeUrPenLOUD is an excellent resource for lifestyle bloggers. Without further adieu, I would like to help you #MakeUrPenLOUD.

Chapter 2: What is a Lifestyle Blogger?

Dear Pennies & Pens,

From day one, I knew I wanted #MakeUrPenLOUD to be totally different from anything else on the market. As you know, I started as a music blogger, and then transitioned to fashion and now lifestyle.

#MakeUrPenLOUD is about lifestyle blogging because in my humble opinion that is one of the hardest types of bloggers to be. Lifestyle bloggers cover multiple different topics at the same time so we are in a league of our own.

Lifestyle bloggers create content that will inspire, motivate, empower, and entertain our readers. Lifestyle bloggers blog about fashion, beauty, music, art, home decor, sports, travel, food, wine, beer, events, etc. Lifestyle blogs are unique because the content is very diverse and ever changing. Lifestyle blogs are written from the perspective of the blogger so no two lifestyle blogs are the same. Lifestyle blogs usually do have a focal point such as music or fashion but overall the content varies.

Lifestyle bloggers write and publish blog posts, shoot images for their blogs and social media, and collaborate with brands. In theory, they do what every blogger does but what makes them different from other niches is they must be multitaskers. A lifestyle blogger has to learn to juggle multiple projects simultaneously. For example, they may have to coordinate a press trip while also writing an album review.

Lifestyle bloggers have to manage several different projects at the same time because their blog must be consistently updated with new content. Since their blogs are lifestyle focused, the blogger has to present diverse content to keep readers engaged.

Lifestyle bloggers are a fusion of the original blogger aka personal bloggers and niche bloggers. When blogging first became popular, most people maintained personal blogs where they wrote about their personal lives, interests, and hobbies.

As the blogging industry grew, someone decided that bloggers should have a niche such as music or fashion. Everyone quickly followed suit and people began to identify themselves as "music bloggers", "fashion bloggers", "beauty bloggers", or "travel bloggers", etc. Each of these bloggers only creates content about things related to their niche.

This is great for the blogger because they only write content about one specific topic. In essence, they become subject matter experts on their topic of choice. However, niche blogging can be frustrating to readers because people with multiple interests must now follow a bunch of different blogs instead of just few.

Personally, I never liked blogging about one topic. I always thought it was boring and when I moved to Texas, I saw that as my opportunity to expand. I liked the idea of being a lifestyle site because it would allow me to cover a range of topics at the same time. In addition, I knew I would be able to reach a broader audience with diverse content. With a site that features fashion, beauty, music, art, travel, and events, I knew that I could appeal to anyone within my target audience. This way, my site would be all inclusive and not discriminate against anyone.

Most bloggers still have a niche, but lately, I have noticed that more and more blogs are covering a wider range of content. The bloggers who are starting to create lifestyle content are mostly former niche bloggers who got bored only blogging about one thing.

This is why I believe lifestyle blogging will be the wave of the future. With a lifestyle blog, neither the blogger nor the reader will get bored. I believe that lifestyle bloggers are important because we are knowledgeable about a variety of topics. Lifestyle bloggers work with an array of brands thereby building a robust rolodex of contacts.

This means we have powerful networks and the ability to execute almost any project. We also have greater influence because different types of people follow us since our blogs feature a unique mixture of content.

Having said that, I truly believe that lifestyle blogging is the way to go. I want you to become a lifestyle blogger so that you can develop a wide range of skills and experiences as I have. With this book, pen, and paper in hand, you will be armed with the tools to #MakeUrPenLOUD.

Chapter 3: How to Find Content for Your Blog

Dear Pennies & Pens,

One of the hardest parts of blogging is finding content for your blog. You have to update your blog consistently in order to build and sustain a dedicated readership. In essence, there's a lot of pressure on bloggers to constantly create new posts.

There are many places where you can look for content to feature on your blog. It is a matter of being able to search different sources and find content that you are passionate about or think is interesting enough to share with your readers. Let's talk about how to find content for your blog.

1. Do research - search Google, blogs, and social media for the latest news and interesting stories that would make great content. I find content by simply always keeping my eyes and ears open for refreshing stories. When I find those stories, I do more research and then write my post.

2. Sign up for press lists - Services like Vocus, MyMediaInfo, and Cision have a "Publisher/Blogger" portal where you can sign up to receive press releases from brands. This is a great way to find content and get the news before anyone else.

Press releases will be delivered right to your email and you can simply read/skim through them and write about the best ones. Note you will receive a TON of releases this way but it is very helpful. Also it'll give you a brand's contact info so you can work with them on future projects.

3. Contact Public Relations Agencies - PR agencies exist to obtain media coverage for their clients. In essence, they are always looking for bloggers who want to write about their clients. If you contact them and ask to be added to their media list, you are making their job that much easier.

You can find PR agencies by searching on google. You can also search Twitter and Instagram as most agencies have presence on social media. Once you do these steps, visit their website and look for an email address.

It's best to look for an email that goes to someone directly like Sue@pragency.com. A direct contact email is best because you're more likely to actually connect with someone. Also try to find out who manages PR for the brand you'd like to work with and contact that person directly.

4. Follow different types of blogs - Follow different types blogs to keep up with what they are covering. Then write posts on the things you like best.

5. Social Media - Follow your favorite brands, bloggers, and people on social media then write about things they are talking about. A brand will always talk about their latest products and services on social media so it's a great way to keep up with them and find content.

6. Brainstorm - Write down a list of topics or concepts that you can write about on your blog. Maybe you can write about your favorite book, movie, or artist. Or you can write your opinion on a hot news topic.

You will find that posts brainstormed by you are the most fun to create because they come from the heart. Also, this is when you can be creative.

I truly believe that the above listed ways will help you find unique content for your blog. It will take a while for you to develop an eye for great content but you will.

Chapter 4: How to Write About Fashion

Dear Pennies & Pens,

Fashion has played a key role in my life. It has been one of the things that set the foundation for who I am today.

My mother and grandmother are both fashion designers; although they never designed for a living, both of them have created many pieces of clothing from scratch. And while they both create patterns, neither of them sketches.

Even though I grew up in a family of fashion lovers, I didn't know that a career in the industry was possible until I was in my 20s and living in NYC. When I started in the industry, I realized there were many facts and terms that I didn't know. To remedy my lack of knowledge, I read many books about fashion as well as following designers, editors, bloggers, stylists, etc. on social media.

Now that I have gained experience writing about fashion, I would love to pass my knowledge onto you. Writing about fashion takes practice, research, and time. Many people view fashion as a something that is frivolous and superficial but in my opinion it is a vital part of life.

Fashion is how we identify someone's financial status, ethnicity, sex, marital status, personal style, and much more. Basically, we classify people based on how they dress. We can also identify a certain period of time base on how people are dressed in photos and art.

In order to write about fashion, there are some things you should do to hone your craft. Below, I have included a list to help you get started.

1. **Do research** - Google designers, brands, stylists, editors, models, and photographers to find out who's who in the industry. You should also visit the library and read as many books about fashion, beauty, and style as you can. Another great way to do research is to watch fashion

documentaries. These films usually focus on the work of an iconic designer and how they built their business.

It is important to become well versed in the industry so people view you as someone who is knowledgeable and is serious about building a career in the industry. As you conduct your research, be sure to take notes so you can keep track of everything.

2. **Learn from the experts** - Take classes and visit websites like Style.com, Women's Wear Daily, Vogue, and Fashionista regularly. Taking classes will help you master the history of fashion and learn how the industry works whereas reading fashion websites and blogs will help you keep up with the latest news.

If you are looking for specific names to help you get started, I recommend checking out Tim Blanks, Cathy Horyn, Robin Givhan, Teri Agins, Andre Leon Talley, Grace Coddington, Yuli Ziv, Dr. Valerie Steele, Diana Vreeland, June Ambrose, and Joe Zee. Each of these people is an industry icon so knowing who they are is a must. Additionally, they will lead you to other people that you should learn about as well.

Another go to resource for fashion insider knowledge is "The Teen Vogue Handbook: The Insider's Guide to Careers in Fashion". This book is an absolute must read for any aspiring blogger. It contains advice and interviews with established fashion influencers. It is very inspiring and motivating.

Studying the work of your established industry peers will help you learn what their stories are as well as their paths to success. This will help you map out your own path and determine your goals. Additionally, you will see that success is not easy to obtain but it is possible.

3. **Learn fashion terms** - I believe that you should learn fashion terms to be able to properly write about fashion and describe clothing and accessories. I recommend reading "The Thames & Hudson Dictionary of Fashion and Fashion Designers" to learn fashion terms.

In order to properly write about fashion and review designers' collections, you need to know what draping is, what a color palette is, and understand the differences between various types of fabric. Knowing industry lingo and the process of creating clothing and accessories will assist you in writing about fashion.

4. **Attend Fashion Shows and Events** -- Attending fashion shows and events will give you the exclusive opportunity to view the latest clothing and accessories months before the average consumer. Fashion Week happens twice a year in New York, London, Paris, and Milan.

Many other cities have a fashion week and other fashion events as well but New York, London, Paris, and Milan are considered the fashion capitals of the world. So if you can, you definitely want to seek to attend a show in one of these places to observe how the pros do it.

However, if you cannot don't fret because you'd be surprised to find that fashion designers are building businesses in other cities due to New York, London, Paris, and Milan all being extremely competitive. Additionally, each city has a high cost of living. Dallas, Austin, Atlanta, Charleston, and Portland are affordable American cities that have a growing fashion industry and events to match.

L.A. and Chicago are also popular cities for fashion, they are pricey as well but it is possible to build a business. Internationally, Copenhagen, Amsterdam, Berlin, Moscow, Hong Kong, and Dubai have major fashion events that are worth checking out if you can.

Scope social media, Google, and blogs to find fashion shows and events. Please refer to the how to attend and cover events chapter for detailed instructions on finding events.

5. **Talk to fashion insiders** - Talk to your industry peers and ask them what they think of a certain designer, collection, or the latest fashion news story. This will give you ideas for your own posts and help you understand the state of the industry.

6. Develop your own eye and style - Figure out what designers and brands excite you and why. Do you like haute couture or classic American sportswear or multicultural fashion?

Once you know what type of fashion you respond to, you can start focusing on featuring those types of designers.

As far as your own personal style, what do you like to wear? Where do you shop? You can write about places you like to shop or your favorite brands. This will help you define your own style and focus your fashion coverage.

7. Practice, practice, practice - Start writing about fashion as often as possible. It will take a while to keep track of everyone who works in the industry as well as all the designers and brands. That said, the sooner you start, the better off you will be.

The cool thing about writing about fashion is that you can do it in different ways. You can interview designers, models, photographers, bloggers, and stylists. You can also review designers' collections and shows. You can also create outfits to recommend to readers for certain events and occasions.

Additionally, you can write about a brand's latest products and collection or talk about their latest news or collaborations. There are many different avenues to explore. Get creative and see what you can come up with.

Chapter 5: How to Attend New York Fashion Week

Dear Pennies & Pens,

In the last chapter, we talked about how to write about fashion. In that chapter, I mentioned attending fashion shows and events like New York Fashion Week.

Since New York Fashion Week is such an exclusive event and New York is one of the world's fashion capitals, I thought it would be best to dedicate an entire chapter on breaking down how to get into America's most fabulous fashion event.

Every season of New York Fashion Week, my business partner Cacha` and I get an email from someone asking us if they can cover New York Fashion Week for us or if we will help get them in. We always joke and say "people act like we're the New York Fashion Week fairy godmothers and we can just grant their wish to attend New York Fashion Week."

Sadly, Cacha` and I aren't magical fairies, we're just hard working women who've been blessed with amazing opportunities. We have a covered a variety of New York Fashion Week events including The Couture Council Luncheon Honoring Valentino and the Daphne Guinness Press Preview at the Museum at FIT. We have also attended shows for designers like Chris Benz, Zang Toi, Carlos Miele, and Sally LaPointe.

I believe that anyone can attend New York Fashion Week but there are some things you must have and do in order to get in. Having said that, let's start with defining what New York Fashion Week is so we can finally answer the question: How to Get into New York Fashion Week.

1. **What is New York Fashion Week?** -- With the influx of blogs and social media, the buzz about New York Fashion Week is at all-time high. But few people understand what it actually is. New York Fashion Week is an exclusive, industry only event held twice a year.

2. **When is New York Fashion Week?** -- New York Fashion Week happens in February and September. February is for the Spring/Summer collections and September is for the Fall/Winter collections.

3. **What is the purpose of New York Fashion Week?** -- The purpose of New York Fashion Week is to create a platform for established and emerging designers to showcase their collections to the media, buyers, stylists, celebrities, and fashion enthusiasts.

4. **Who can attend New York Fashion Week?** -- Just to reiterate, New York Fashion Week is an industry only event which means only those who work in fashion can attend. That said bloggers, editors, and photographers a.k.a. "the media", buyers, celebrities, and fashion enthusiasts can attend New York Fashion Week.

5. **Why do people attend New York Fashion Week and what role do they play?**

The Media attends New York Fashion Week to cover the shows for the various publications or outlets they work for.

Editors attend fashion week to observe the collections, offer designers feedback, and look for pieces to feature in future issues of the magazine they work for. Editors impact New York Fashion Week because they are so powerful!

Editors have the power to propel a designer's career because the publications they work for have enormous budgets to produce dramatic editorials featuring the designer's work.

Additionally, they have a massive network of influential contacts who can offer support to the designer. The support of an editor can make or a break a designer.

Bloggers attend fashion week to create online content about fashion week and do live coverage of the shows via social media. Bloggers are the reason that New York Fashion Week has been able to sustain relevance in the digital world. Bloggers create online hype and social buzz about fashion week because they make everyone who is not at the shows feel like they were there by live tweeting and instagramming throughout the shows.

People love bloggers because most started as everyday people with an interest in fashion, who rose to become industry trendsetters. In essence, people trust the opinion of bloggers and view it as more authentic and real than that of an editor.

Bloggers also play a major role at fashion week by discovering emerging designers. Bloggers love unearthing new designers and will often feature new designers on their blogs months or years before the designer "blows up".

I covered Rubin Singer's New York Fashion Week show in 2010 and Beyoncé` wore Rubin Singer for her 2013 Super Bowl performance. In essence, bloggers like me help put emerging designers on the map.

Photographers attend New York Fashion Week to shoot photos of the collections, street style, and the various events. Photographers play an extremely important role because their images act as a recording of the shows, events, and looks shown.

Photographers are necessary to the success of New York Fashion Week because their images capture the essence of the event.
Editors, stylists, bloggers, buyers, all need high quality images of the shows in order to create content, write reviews, decide which pieces to buy, and what to feature in editorials. That said images are a must.

Influential photographers can impact a designer's career because their images could capture the interest of a top editor, blogger, or stylist which will further propel the designer. Top photographers are also very well connected and can recommend using a designer's pieces which would help build brand awareness for the designer.

28

Photographers usually work for publications or they are freelancers. If a photographer works for a publication they have been assigned to shoot photos of the shows; if they are freelance they simply attend shows (and shoot street style looks) in hopes that an editor or blogger will chose their photos and publish their work.

Buyers attend New York Fashion Week to look for clothing accessories to purchase for their retail stores or boutiques. Buyers usually work for major retailers like Nordstrom, Bergdorf Goodman, Macy's, Barneys, or independent boutiques.
Buyers are important because this is when the registers start ringing! Designers love buyers because they are the people who support their work financially.

A large order can give a designer enough money to sustain or expand their business. Every buyer is different and the store they work for (or own) determines the type of clothing and accessories they will buy.

Most buyers are looking for pieces that their consumer will buy so they make a profit. If you are a designer this important to know so you don't try to sell a buyer pieces they won't buy.

Stylists attend New York Fashion Week to look for pieces to "pull" aka borrow for various projects. There are two types of stylists: editorial and celebrity.

Editorial stylists work for print or online publications and they are responsible for coordinating looks for editorials. Editorials are fashion shoots that will be published in a magazine or on a blog.

When attending fashion week, an editorial stylist usually has a concept they are seeking to bring to life through a shoot. That said they are attending fashion week to find pieces that will make the concept real. Editorial stylists can be very powerful because pieces pulled by them could end up being a 4 page Vogue spread or going viral online.

Celebrity stylists create looks for their clients to wear to events, performances, and general everyday wear. Because of blogs and social media, celebrities are constantly being photographed thereby increasing the pressure to always look good and be stylish. That said, most celebrities hire a stylist to create outfits for them.

Celebrity stylists attend New York Fashion Week to find the latest designer frocks to dress their clients in. A celebrity stylist's client list determines the pieces they are looking to pull. Each of their clients has a certain style or image they are looking to portray so their stylist will only pull pieces that illustrate that.

Celebrity stylists are important because their pulls could end up on an A list actress, actor, or musician resulting in enormous exposure for the designer. Certain celebrities have been the cause of designer pieces selling out in stores and online.

Models, designers, misc. Models attend fashion week to walk the runways during the shows or to check out the collections. Designers will attend other designers' shows to support their work or observe how a more established designer presents a collection.

Celebrities attend fashion week to be seen...plain and simple. Some are also there to support their designer friends or because they are truly interested in fashion but 8 times out of 10, celebs attend the shows to promote their latest project.

Now that we have talked about everyone who attends New York Fashion Week and identified all their roles, let's finally talk about how to get in!

How to Attend Into New York Fashion Week

1. Write about fashion - You would be surprised at the number of emails I receive from people who don't even have a blog let alone write about fashion who want to attend fashion week. I'm honestly lost as to why people who have shown no serious interest in fashion think they should be invited to shows.

Moving right along, the first thing I recommend to attend New York Fashion Week is to have a blog that features fashion. Writing about fashion on your blog will showcase your skills and knowledge of the industry. It will show that you are serious about fashion and are not there for the glitz and glamour.

2. Build relationships with Public Relations Agencies - In regards to New York Fashion Week, PR agencies are responsible for creating the guest list and seating arrangements. In some cases, PR agencies are also responsible for planning the show itself.

PR girls should be your BFF!!! I love publicists and PR agencies, they are the liaison between me (a blogger) and their client (a designer) so they help make articles happen. They send me press releases, images, and anything else I need to write and publish great posts.

That said, you should definitely build relationships with PR reps. The way to do that is to email them, introduce yourself, and ask to be added to their press list. You should do this at least few months before fashion week. This way you start building a relationship sooner than later.

Once you receive a press release or pitch from that PR rep, feature it on your blog, then email them the link. They will appreciate your thoughtfulness and the blog mention. This will make them more likely to extend you an invite to their client's next New York Fashion Week show.

To find PR agencies, search on Google or visit designers' websites and look for the PR contact info. Tip: Google "designer name pr contact" or "designer name website" or "fashion pr agencies in nyc"; one of those searches should lead you in the right direction.

3. Email PR Agencies To Request Invites - Please note the only way to attend a New York Fashion Week show is to be invited. Invites are sent by designers' PR teams so if you want to attend a particular designer's show, email their publicist and request to be added to the guest list.

In your email, introduce yourself and your blog (be sure to include a link to your blog and/or media kit). Then tell them why you would like to attend the designer's show.

Keep this email brief as PR reps are extremely busy and don't have time to read a 4 page letter email. It helps if you have already featured the designer on your blog because it makes your request more authentic.

4. Collaborate or intern with established bloggers - Established bloggers make the perfect people to collaborate with! They have been where you are and most importantly they need help. They are getting invited to more shows than they can personally attend so they need assistance covering shows.

Email established bloggers introducing yourself and telling them why you want to work with them. Keep it real by giving them honest compliments do not just kiss their behind.

If they agree to work with you show them you are serious by actually going to the shows you are supposed to cover, then writing posts on the shows, as well as taking a few photos.

When you work with another blogger, you are there to represent their blog and brand. That means you should be promoting them and making sure everyone knows who you work for.

Also, you should connect with the blogger you would like to partner with months or weeks before New York Fashion Week. Do not email someone the week of or day before begging to get into a show and expect a handout. Handouts are for the homeless sweetie.

5. Get Invites: If you have shown a serious interest in fashion, you will receive invites to New York Fashion Week shows and events without asking for them. This is the best feeling ever!

Since New York Fashion Week is an industry only event the fact that someone has invited you to cover their show means they value your blog and your opinion.

You should feel honored and appreciated that someone has definitely recognized your work in a positive way.

6. Attend shows and events - Once you receive invites, be sure to RSVP and actually attend the shows.

PR agencies and designers track who attends their shows so you don't want to look like Nancy no-show. The more shows and events you cover the more you will be invited to.

7. Write about the shows and events - Write about the shows and events you attend during fashion week because other PR agencies or designers could find your coverage and extend an invite to their show next season.

Everyone is always looking for more bloggers to cover their shows so the more fashion week events you feature, the more you'll get invited to.

Chapter 6: How to Plan Fashion and Lifestyle Photoshoots

Dear Pennies & Pens,

In the last couple of chapters, we talked about how to write about fashion and how to attend New York Fashion Week. Now, let's talk about how to plan fashion and lifestyle photo shoots for your blog.

Once published, fashion and lifestyle photoshoots are often referred to as editorials. A fashion or lifestyle editorial is about bringing a certain concept, theme, or idea to life through images shot during a photo shoot.

A fashion editorial focuses on showcasing the clothing and accessories whereas a lifestyle editorial features people in real life situations captured in an artistic way. Both types of editorials focus on selling through imagery.

Creating fashion and lifestyle editorials will give you unique and original images for your blog and social media outlets. It's important to have your own original images so you can showcase your creative talents and promote yourself as well as your work.

Planning fashion and lifestyle photoshoots is a tedious process because there are so many elements involved. Since the process of planning photo shoots is so complex, I have broken it down step by step.

Coordinating Your Shoot

1. **Find & book a photographer** - Before you can shoot one fashion or lifestyle editorial, you must first secure a photographer. You can either take your own photos using a camera and tripod, have a friend or family member take the photos, or hire a photographer.

Everyone has a different situation so do what works best for you. The biggest piece of advice I can offer is to make sure that the final product is awesome. Trust and believe no one cares who shot the images, people just want to see high quality, original photography.

I will say that working with a photographer simplifies the process of shooting because you know you are going to be working with a professional who knows how to shoot and edit photos.

Also, a professional photographer usually has all the equipment needed to execute a shoot not to mention experience. If you decide to work with a professional photographer, you will have to compensate them for their time or work out a trade/barter agreement.

To find a photographer, check out other fashion and lifestyle blogs to see who's shooting their photos. When you discover out the photographer's name, Google them, visit their website and contact them about collaborating. You can also conduct a general Google search, search social media (specifically Twitter, Instagram, Tumblr) to find photographers in your area.

On the other hand, shooting your own photos cuts out the middleman entirely. With this option, you would have full control over when and where the shoot takes place as well as how the photos are edited. This means you don't have to depend on anyone. If you are a control freak like me this option probably seems pretty appealing.

The last resort is to have a friend or family member shoot your photos. I call this a last resort because unless it is someone who has a genuine interest in photography, it is usually not a good idea. Family and friends may not understand how serious this project is to you meaning they could be inconsistent or not serious about working with you.

This could lead to them not showing up to shoots, not editing photos as promised, etc. If you have a family member or friend who is an aspiring photographer, then by all means take advantage. However, don't think you can walk up to any of your family members hand them a camera and expect them to magically become a photographer.

2. **Work out details with the photographer -** Now that you have found a photographer, you need to hash out the details. Will you be paying the photographer or bartering services? If you are paying, decide on an

amount that works for you both. Also, determine when and how the photographer will be paid.

If you are bartering, decide what you will be trading, maybe they will shoot your photos in exchange for social media marketing. It is important to negotiate the payment or barter terms early so there is no confusion later.

Next, decide what day you will be shooting and the time. You should also discuss concepts and themes for the shoot. Tell the photographer why you are shooting and what you want to accomplish. Also provide a bio that tells the photographer who you are and why you started blogging. These details will give the photographer a sense of who you are. Knowing more about you helps them shoot you better.

After this, you and the photographer should determine the location. You should definitely have some locations in mind, but, you should allow the photographer to provide input on location because they understand lighting and logistics.

The last detail to be finalized is what type of shoot it is and how you will execute it. If the shoot is for a fashion editorial, you and the photographer should finalize how many looks (outfits) you will be shooting.

If it is a lifestyle editorial, ask yourself what real life event are you seeing to recreate for this editorial, then figure out what props, clothing, or location you will need to make the editorial work. Once you do that, finalize the details with the photographer so you are both on the same page.

3. Decide on a concept or theme - Fashion editorials are usually inspired by film, TV, travel, people, a particular piece of clothing or accessory, period of time, etc. Lifestyle editorials are inspired by real life events.

To decide on a concept or theme, look for inspiration and brainstorm ideas. For fashion editorials, think about movies you have seen, music you've heard, your favorite designer, a period of time you relate to, etc.

Look closely at the clothes and accessories, and ask yourself: "do I have similar pieces? Or is there some way I can recreate those looks?" Fashion editorials can also be about showcasing your personal style. Go through your closet and pull out your favorite pieces. Which pieces communicate who you are and what you like to wear?

For lifestyle editorials, think about the real life events you are seeking to depict in photos. Since you are a blogger, let's use that as an example. Think about having the photographer shoot you while you use your laptop, tablet, and phone to write posts and create content for social media.

This could be a cool lifestyle shoot because it could inspire your readers who may be aspiring bloggers to finally start their blogs. Seeing you blog will motivate them and show them how it's done. To make the photos more artistic, have the photographer shoot close-ups of what's on your screen, what you're wearing, etc.

Concepts and themes centralize the shoot and keep you focused so they are an extremely important. Keep in mind that when people see the final photos they are supposed to understand and see concept just by looking at the photo. If you have to explain it, you missed the mark.

4. Choose a location - When you are selecting a location for your shoot, you have to be strategic and smart. The location is meant to enhance and complement the concept/theme of the shoot. Decide if you will be shooting outside, in a studio, or on location.

Outside shoots are great because the background is always interesting and can add character to your photos. Studio shoots are dope because it is private and you have complete control over lighting, can play music, not to mention, there is a place to change and do hair and makeup.

On location shoots are cool too because they make the photos look unique or exotic. I did an on location shoot with my photographer Megan Mueller at the Omni Dallas and the photos looked amazing! We shot the pictures in my hotel room and it really added character to the photos.

I recommend you chose a location based on the weather, your budget, and schedule. Figure out what will work best for you and then execute.

5. Decide who will star in the shoot - Will you be the star of the shoot or will you be working with a model, artist, entrepreneur, friend, or family member who will be starring in the shoot?

The person in the photos will determine what will be worn in the shoot. It is important to note this because you have to make sure your subject will look good and feel confident in what they are wearing/doing.

If you are working with a subject, make sure you do everything in your power to make sure the subject is prepared for the shoot. That could range from giving instructions on how they should pose, what they should wear, hair, makeup, etc. Never assume that your subject has experience shooting even if they are a model, artist, blogger, or entrepreneur because it could come back to bite you in the behind.

If you are the subject of the shoot, practice your facial expressions and poses in the mirror. Take selfies to see when you look your best and when you don't. This exercise will help you understand how your face and body looks in photos so you know what poses or facial expression to make during your shoot.

Overall, knowing who will be the subject of your shoot is crucial to coordinating a shoot because it affects how the shoot will happen.

6. Create and Style the looks - Now it is time to create and style the looks that will be worn for the shoot. Please note you will be styling the looks based on the concept, theme, and subject of the shoot.

As I said earlier, fashion editorials focus on the clothes and accessories so the looks for these shoots must be on point. For lifestyle editorials, clothes and accessories should be realistic in the aspect that it's what someone in that position would wear.

There are a couple ways to create and style the looks for your shoot. You can use your subject's pieces or your own, go shopping, or collaborate with a designer or brand to use their pieces.

With your own clothes & accessories, simply go through your closet and pick out pieces that fit your shoot's concept and theme. For a shoot with another subject, schedule a time to go to their house and raid their closet. You need items they look good in and that will work your shoot.

If there's something you need for your shoot but do not have then go shopping. While shopping, be sure to stay focused because you are there for a purpose. Only go to stores that have what you need, if you are unsure research them online first and then make an in person visit. Shopping can get expensive so only buy items that you will be able to reuse.

If you would like to pull (borrow) items from a brand or designer for your shoot, then you will need to contact them. Please refer to chapter 7, "How to Collaborate with Fashion and Beauty Brands" for instructions on requesting clothing and accessories from designers.

7. Finalize hair & makeup - Once you figure out the clothes and accessories, you need to decide how hair and makeup will be done. Hair and makeup should complement the clothes and accessories as well as the shoot's concept and location.

With hair and makeup, there are some things you should keep in mind. The texture and color of the subject's hair as well as their ethnicity and complexion will affect what styles can be done to their hair and what kind of makeup they can wear.

You also need to figure out who will do the hair and makeup. If you or your subject cannot do it look into booking a makeup artist or hair stylist. You or your subject can also go to a salon and have a stylist do the hair in the predetermined style.

8. Do a fitting - Before your shoot do a fitting for yourself or your subject. Have all the clothes and accessories there so that everything can be tried on. Make sure you have a mirror to check everything out as well as a camera to capture how everything looks.

The fitting is when you should finalize what will actually be worn at the shoot. Although you have done your homework, you will find that some items just will not work and should be pulled from the shoot.

9. Pack for your shoot - I recommend packing clothing and accessories by type or look. This will help you stay organized and make it easier to execute the shoot. To pack by type, pack the shirts, dresses, pants, jewelry, shoes, etc. separately and label them. This way everything is together and you know what each bag contains.

To pack by look, pack the top, pants, shoes, accessories together and label it as "Look 1", "Look 2", etc. This way you will be able to pull out each look one at a time. Packing is about being organized so your shoot goes off without a hitch. There is nothing worse than having to search for things when you're in the middle of a shoot.

8. Plan logistics - Figure out how you or your subject will get to your shoot, how you will get the clothes and accessories to your shoot, and where hair and makeup will be done. It is important to do this before your shoot so everything runs smoothly. Shooting is stressful enough without you adding to it.

9. Follow-Up - Follow up with your photographer and subject (if you have one) to confirm the shoot date and time. This allows you to make any last minute changes, etc. prior to the shoot.

Executing Your Shoot

1. Arrive early or on time - On the day of your shoot, make sure you arrive early or on time. You want to show your photographer and subject that you are serious about what you do. This will make them want to work with you again. Arriving late throws everything off and makes you feel disorganized.

I made this mistake once and it was such a buzzkill! My photographer did not hold it against me but I felt so rushed and I didn't like that. Not to mention that at the end of the shoot, we lost daylight which could've been detrimental. However, we worked through it and the photos came out great but I vowed to never make that mistake again.

2. Start getting dressed and doing hair & makeup - Getting dressed and doing hair and makeup can get quite time consuming. This is why you should start as soon as possible. My business partner and I made this key mistake on our first shoot.
We spent too much time doing hair and makeup and not enough time shooting. The end result was that we did not shoot all the clothes we pulled and of course we fought about it. Since then, we have learned how to execute shoots so I'm hoping you'll learn from our mistakes.

3. Chat with your photographer and subject before shooting to discuss poses, lighting, and the specific location -- Once you get to the shoot, tell the photographer your ideas for poses and listen to their input about poses and lighting. After that, you guys should meet somewhere in the middle and begin executing.

If you are shooting a subject, I do not recommend consulting them about poses unless they have experience shooting and you think you will like their ideas. They may be starring in your shoot but it is your shoot so

41

have to have full creative control. Also keep in mind the old adage of "too many cooks in the kitchen".

Lastly, even though you already have a location, you need to choose a specific area within your location. This means decide what side of the room or what spot you will be shooting in.

4. Starting shooting and have fun - Now that all the prep work is finally done, you can start shooting! Be sure to try out different poses to see what works best in photos. If you are working with a subject, guide and direct them during the shoot.

Make sure your subject is comfortable so that they are confident and take great photos. If you are the subject of your shoot, have fun with it and do not think about it too much.

5. Let the photographer guide you or your subject - Your photographer is behind the camera so they know what poses make you or your subject look cool, awkward, indifferent, etc.
That said listen to them when they make suggestions! You want the images to look awesome so accept feedback and act accordingly.

After the shoot

1. Wait for the rough images - The photographer will send you the unedited images for you to choose the final images.

2. Sort through the images and pick your favorites - Now that you have the unedited images, you have to go through all of them and choose which ones will be edited.

I must admit that I hate doing this because it is so tedious! Sometimes the only difference between two photos is the angle, lighting, or the pose. Either way, this is a must for you to identify the best images that will be edited and published to your blog. When making your selections, be sure to choose a variety of photos so you have photos to use on the blog and social media.

3. Send images to be edited to the photographer - Now that you have picked out your favorites, send them to the photographer to be edited. Once you get them back, you can move onto the last and final step!

4. Publish the editorials - Depending on what type of editorials you shot, determines how you should publish them to your blog.

I recommend that in the post(s), you either only publish the photos and let the images speak for themselves or tell a story about the photos as far as what you or the subject is wearing, when and where the images were shot, the shoot concept, etc.

With fashion editorials, I usually publish one look at a time to spread out the content. For Lifestyle editorials, I publish all the photos at once with text that explains the photos.

In general, I usually publish written stories with my photos. I like to tell a story about my photos because it makes it more interesting and relatable. When it comes to publishing your editorials, I think you should do what works best for you. It is more important to be yourself and be authentic with your audience. I think you should let your creative juices flow and the rest will work itself out.

Chapter 7: How to Collaborate with Fashion and Beauty Brands

Dear Pennies & Pens,

I have learned that collaborating with fashion and beauty brands is a true art form. It is a business transaction where you will be exchanging goods and in some cases money. With brand collaborations, each party brings something to the table to create a final product.

In the case of blogging collaborations, the blogger offers their knowledge, audience, and creative talents while a brand offers a product or financial support. Both parties have something that the other needs but each party will have to compromise in order to make the project work.

Usually, working with fashion or beauty brands results in two types of posts product reviews or editorials (created after shooting the pieces during a photo shoot). In order to create this type of content, the blogger must request the product or a sample...this process is called a sample request. After the brand receives and approves the request, they send the product (free of charge) to the blogger to be reviewed or shot. The blogger then creates their content and either returns or keeps the product.

Please note, beauty samples are never returned since that is unsanitary. It varies on whether or not samples are returned to fashion brands because this happens at the brand's discretion. A brand may send a blogger a sample to shoot but the sample must be returned within a certain time frame.

In this case, the brand only allows the blogger to borrow or "pull" the piece for a limited amount of time because they want the piece to be shot by other bloggers, stylists, editors, etc. However, if the blogger is established and has a major following, the brand may allow the blogger to keep the items.

Fashion and beauty brands like to get their products in the hands of bloggers because the content is more original and interactive. Upon receiving the product, the blogger can take photos of it to upload to Instagram, shoot a video tutorial or review, or does a photo shoot featuring the product.

I have worked with a variety of fashion and beauty brands such as Macy's, Rimmel London, Derma e, Perlier, Durrah Jewellery, Real Techniques, Vionic, Diamondere, Clayspray, Ouidad, and Thirty-One Gifts. Naturally, I have learned the process of collaborating with brands and would love to share my knowledge with you.

1. Create a list - Write a list of fashion and beauty brands that you would like to work with. Your list should include brands that have products you would actually wear, use, or buy (if you have not already done so). Working with fashion and beauty brands is inherently creative process so you want it to be real and authentic.

2. Do research - Do research on the brands you want to work with.

For fashion brands, you need to know who the designer or creative director is and their bio, where the brand's flagship store is, if the brand sells online, who their target customer is, the price point, what stores the clothing or accessories are sold in, and if they present their latest collections at fashion week.

For beauty brands, you need to know more about the founder or manufacturer, the type of products the brand makes (makeup, skincare, haircare), where the products are made (in US or abroad), how the products are made (are they all natural or do they contain chemicals), the price point, where the products are sold (in stores and/or online), who the target customer is, and where the brand is located.

3. Connect with the brand via social media - Lately, I have noticed that fashion and beauty brands want to work with bloggers who are already following them on social media. This is because they believe that bloggers who follow them on social media are genuinely interested in their brand and are not just approaching them for free products or money.

Follow the brand on social media, and like, RT, or comment on some of their posts regularly. This can help in getting their attention and building a relationship with them. Also, this will help you stay up to date on what they have going on so it is definitely a must.

4. Prepare your pitch - When it comes to working with fashion and beauty brands, there are a few things that you need to present in order to land the project. For fashion brands, you will need to send a Letter of Responsibility (LOR) and an editorial pull request.

A **letter of responsibility or a "pull letter"** is a document in which the blogger assumes responsibility for the return and safekeeping of all items borrowed. The pull letter should also state that designers and brands will be credited in stories published on the blog. A letter of responsibility was originally a document for stylists but now that bloggers pull clothing and accessories for shoots as well, they should have their own LOR.

An **editorial pull request** is a document that I created to streamline the process of pitching projects to brands. The editorial pull request includes all the details of the shoot and project.

My editorial pull request includes:
- my contact information (name, email, phone number)
- a link to my website
- a link to my styling portfolio
- a link to the photographer's portfolio
- the name of the editorial
- the date of the shoot, the shoot location, the pulling date (the day I want to pick up or receive the clothes/accessories)
- the return date (the day all items will be returned)

46

- the purpose of the pull request (why I need the clothes/accessories)
- the concept of the shoot (my creative ideas and concepts).

As far as beauty brands, you need to present product reviews that you have published in order to receive product samples. As previously stated, beauty samples are never returned since that is unsanitary.

That said, when a brand sends a blogger a sample, it is an investment. Therefore, you should send the brand links to previously published reviews so they can verify who you are and what you do. Preparing your pitches will be time consuming when you first start out but you will get the hang of it after a while. Once you create an LOR and the editorial pull request, all you will have to do is update each document for new projects. For beauty brands, you can use the same links over and over again.

5. Contact the publicist, designer, or founder - Most fashion and beauty brands have a publicist who is responsible for managing all press sample requests, building relationships with bloggers, writing press releases, pitching the brand to the media, etc.

If the brand does not have a publicist, it is usually because the brand is new and cannot afford one. In this case, you should contact the designer or founder of the brand directly. The best way to contact the publicist, designer, or founder is to send them an email.

In the email, you should introduce yourself and your blog, provide more information on your target audience (age, location, income level, ethnicity, etc.), as well as your blog and social media stats. All this information should be in your media kit so to save time, you can just send that.

After you introduce yourself and your blog, offer details on your story idea. Tell the brand how you will shoot the clothes or accessories, where the content will be published (on your blog and/or social media), and when the content will be published.

6. Be prepared to compromise and negotiate - Every brand is different but trust there will be something that you will have to compromise on or negotiate to make the project happen.

Sometimes samples will not be available or you will have to travel to get the items. This is totally normal so don't get frustrated when things don't work out exactly as you have planned.

8. **Publish the post(s) -** After you land the collaboration, publish post(s). Please refer to Chapter 4, "how to write about fashion", Chapter 6 "how to plan fashion and lifestyle shoots", and Chapter 8, "How to create beauty posts" to learn the process of publishing fashion and beauty content.

9. **Follow-up with the brand -** After you publish the post(s), be sure to email the link to the publicist, designer, or founder.

Be sure to thank them for choosing to work with you. You should also share the link on your social media and tag the brand in those posts so they see them.

Chapter 8: How to Create Beauty Posts

Dear Pennies & Pens,

Many people visit lifestyle blogs to learn about beauty products. To create beauty posts that people read, you have to be informative, knowledgeable, and entertaining. There are different types of beauty posts, the most popular being product reviews and makeup tutorials.

These types of beauty posts perform well because consumers tend to research products online before purchasing them. They will check out blogs to get insight on how a product works.

Consumers also seek advice from bloggers to decide whether or not they should purchase a product. Additionally, consumers love tutorials because they want to learn how to use products from knowledgeable bloggers.

As a blogger, it is important that you understand how to create beauty posts so that readers find value in your blog. This will make them become regular readers and they will recommend your blog to others.

In this chapter, I will be teaching you how to create beauty posts via product reviews since that is a hard skill to master. Beauty product reviews can be published to your blog as a combination of photos and text or as a video.

I recommend that you use both methods and determine what works best for you. Below, I have outlined both methods. Please note the first four steps are the same for both types of posts.

How to Prepare for your Beauty Product Review:

1. Determine the product(s) you will be reviewing - Will you be reviewing makeup, skin care, or a hair care product? The type of product determines how you should approach your review.

Makeup is supposed to enhance facial features or cover blemishes. Skin care products are designed to cleanse the face or address certain concerns like wrinkles or acne. Hair care products vary in what they do but they are mostly created to improve hair's appearance or make it grow.

2. Use the product multiple times - Using the product multiple times will give you time to see how it affects you. During this time, you will develop an opinion of the product and establish whether or not it delivered on its promise.

3. Take notes - Take notes on how the product affected you. Did the product cause your skin to breakout? How did it smell? How did it feel?

You can also take notes on details about the product such as the packaging, price, and manufacturer. All these notes can be referenced in your final video review.

4. Do research - Visit the manufacturer's website to learn more about the product. Also read product reviews written by consumers and other bloggers. Not only will you learn more about the product, you get firsthand insight on how the general public and other bloggers feel about the product.

How to Create a Video Review

1. Write a script or make a list of talking points - To create a video review, you should write a script or make a list of talking points before shooting your video to help you stay organized. This way you make sure you cover everything you want to discuss in your video.

Without a script or talking points, you could end up repeating the same points over and over, saying "uh" too many times, or forgetting to include important facts.

I usually write talking points instead of a script because with scripts I end up reading from the page which is not engaging at all. By writing talking points, I stay on track but I still sound authentic and real.

If you write a script, you should memorize it prior to shooting your video. While shooting your video, be sure to make eye contact with the camera and sound excited in the video.

2. Shoot Your Video - Use a high quality camera or webcam to shoot your video. The tool that you use to shoot your video is not as important as the final quality of the video. As long as the final video is high quality viewers don't care how it was shot. Personally, I have used my iPhone and webcam to shoot videos.

Before shooting your video, make sure you have good lighting and that you look presentable. The worse thing that can happen is you shoot a video and no one can see you because the room is too dark.

Also, you do not want to look like a hot mess in the video so be sure your hair is combed and your outfit is flyy. No one is going to trust a beauty review from someone who looks like "Who done it and what for?" Lol!

Start the video by introducing yourself and your blog. I usually just say "It's ya girl LoudPen, Editor of de la Pen...All Pen Everything. Check me out on allpeneverything.com" It's a simple intro and includes info on how viewers can find me online.

Next, provide information on the product and the brand who manufactured it. This makes you look knowledgeable and like you have done your homework. After you do that, talk about what you liked and didn't like about the product. Also include details on how you used the product.

Before you end your video, reiterate all of your talking points including your intro. It is important to remind people of what they've just seen because people have such short attention spans. Repeating yourself will help people commit your review to memory.

How to Create a Photo and Text Review

1. Take photos of the product - Upon purchasing a new beauty product or receiving a product from a brand, take photos of the product. Since your review is a combination of photos and text, your photos are a key element of the post.

You should take photos of the product unopened and unused so readers can see the packaging and the product. Next, take photos of yourself using the product. These photos allow readers to see the product in use. The photos that you take should be used on social media and in your final blog post. I only recommend using your own photos in your final blog post if the photos are high quality.

2. Write the text of your review - Start the post by identifying the product, where it can be purchased, who manufactures it, etc. After that state your opinion of the product and how you used it. When writing, be creative, informative, and interesting.

3. Include photos of the product with your review - Include photos of the product with your review. You can also insert photos of yourself using the product to illustrate your words.

To reiterate, beauty product reviews can be a combination of photos and text or a video. Both types require multiple steps and neither is easier than the other.

Again, I recommend that you experiment with both methods to determine what works better for you. Like everything else, it will take you some time to get the process down but once you do, it will become second nature to you.

Chapter 9: How to Write About Music

Dear Pennies & Pens,

In this chapter, I will be teaching you how to write about music. If you are a music lover like me, you love talking about music and sharing your favorite albums with friends and family. Now that you have a lifestyle blog, you can write about music on your blog. This will give you the chance to be creative, share your opinion, and reach an even broader audience.

As a music aficionado, I am sure you have your fair share of opinions on music and popular artists. However, there is a true art to writing about music. The most popular way of writing about music is to create album reviews.

I have written album reviews of Miley Cyrus' Bangerz, Melanie Fiona's The MF Life, The Weeknd's Trilogy, Little Mix's Salute, and Neon Jungle's Welcome to the Jungle. Writing an album review is tricky because there's no right or wrong way to do it. However, there is a method that will make you more successful so that your reviews are taken seriously. Follow the list below for tips on writing album reviews.

1. Listen to the album multiple times - Personally, I leave an album in rotation for at least a month prior to writing a review. Listening to the album for a while prior to writing and publishing a review helps you get familiar with the album.

To me, music is art that is meant to be digested and interpreted. Listen to the album from beginning to end, from end to the front, and skip certain songs. This will make you hear the album in different ways and you will find yourself catching lyrics you missed on the first go round or a dope solo that is even better than you thought.

You should also listen to the album at different times of day and when you are in different moods. You will find the time of day and your mood can affect how you feel about an album. Please note, these tips are

designed to take the routine out of listening to an album so that you are able to truly hear it.

2. Do research and get the details - Do research to learn the artist's name, which producer created the various records, who wrote the songs, and where the album was recorded.

It is good to know where the album was recorded it gives you a background for how the project came together. It is also helpful to know if this is the artist's first album, what label they are signed to or if they are independent.

Additional biographical details can include the artist's age, where they grew up, where they went to school, etc. These details help you understand the artist which you need to know if you want to write a proper review.

3. Analyze your thoughts and feelings - Think about the songs that you liked, loved, or were indifferent to. Seek to understand why you liked or didn't like certain songs.

Were the lyrics weak, was the beat sick, or did the singer impress you with their vocal ability? What did you think of the album overall? Did each song flow together nicely or was it disjointed?

An album is meant to be a body of work so each song should fit together like pieces of a puzzle, if they do not the album needs work. Analyze how the album made you feel, were you happy, sad, confused? Did the album feature up-tempo tracks that made you want to dance or slow jams that made you want to cuddle with your boo?

Understanding your thoughts and feelings about the album helps you be more creative when writing your post. Understanding your thoughts and feelings will assist you in differentiating your review from others.

4. Take notes - Take notes while listening to the album and doing research. I highly recommend this if you do not have the best memory or want to refer back to certain pieces of information.

Note taking is the key to writing blog posts because you can jot down facts and figures to be referenced later. Once you start writing your post, you can refer back to your notes and include certain pieces in your review.

5. Write your album review - Now the fun begins. Writing an album review is truly an artistic process because as I said earlier, there is no right or wrong answer.

As a blogger, you are critiquing an album based off of your own thoughts, experiences, and interpretation of the album. Some people will agree with your review while others will not.

What separates a good review from a bad one is the ability to clearly communicate your opinion. As far as the format of your post, go with the flow. Do what feels right.

Don't think about it too much. You are creating art about art so have fun with it. Sometimes you may want to start the post by talking about how you discovered the album, why you like the artist, how you felt the first time you listened to it, etc.

Other times you can start by stating the facts such as the artist's name, the album name, how the project was created, etc. If you are a fashion lover like me, you can talk about how much you love the artist's style or the visuals in their last music video.

The most important thing to do is give the reader your thoughts on the album. The reader is looking to you for guidance because they are either

looking for new music to check out or they want insight on an album they are thinking of buying. Your review could be what persuades or dissuades them from purchasing the album.

In regards to stating your opinion, be clear, thorough, yet succinct. I know that may sound like oxymoron but online readers lack patience so they tend to do more scanning than reading. That said readers should be able to decipher whether or not you liked an album very quickly.

Chapter 10: How to Write About Films

Dear Pennies & Pens,

I love movies because I truly believe that the right film can inspire, entertain, and educate you. There are a variety of films like Not Another Happy Ending, Love Jones, Mahogany, Pillow Talk, In A World, The Way Way Back, and The To Do List featured on de la Pen...All Pen Everything.

In this chapter, I will be teaching you how to write about films. The most popular way to write about films is to review them. I have found that the key to writing a quality film review requires that you follow a formula. Below, I have outlined how to write a film review below.

1. Watch the film - This first step would seem obvious but you would be surprised at how many people think they can write a quality blog post without having seen what they are reviewing.

The purpose of a review is to write your opinion on the subject matter, if you have never experienced something, you cannot review it. To me, it is just that simple.

2. Learn the details - Who are the actors and actresses starring in the film? What is the title? Does the title indicate the premise or plot of the movie or show?

What is the plot? Is it meant to be a comedy, drama, or documentary? Is there a narrator? Where is the movie set...in the US or is it international? Who directed and wrote the screenplay?

Learning these details gives you insight on the film which will help greatly when writing your review. You definitely want to include these details in your final post so you give the reader information aka provide value and give them a reason to read your post.

3. Analyze your thoughts and feelings - After you watched the movie, how did you feel? Were you happy, sad, or angry? Did the film or show

give you more knowledge on a subject you didn't know much about? Did the movie make you think? If you liked the movie, why did you like it? Was it because it made you laugh or cry? Was it the beautiful setting of the movie or show, or was it the costumes that you found to be gorgeous?

Understanding your thoughts and feelings on the movie or show helps you determine if you will be writing a positive or negative review. I personally do not recommend writing a completely negative review, if you disliked it that much it is not worth the time or effort.

However, analyzing your thoughts and feelings will help you make the post more personal. People read blogs because they want to connect with a real and authentic voice. So be that voice! To be that voice you have to organize your own thoughts and feelings so you can properly communicate that with your audience.

4. Write your review: Now that you have completed the first three steps, it is time to write your actual review. Start the post with writing the facts, such as the title of the film, director's name, screenwriter's name, and the starring actors' names.

Expand on that with more details such as where the film or show was shot, if it's a comedy or drama, the plot, etc. Lastly, talk about what you liked and didn't like about the film or show. You can also talk about how you came across the film or TV show, why you wanted to write about it, etc. When writing your post, be as creative as possible.

As a lifestyle blogger, you have to understand that people are coming to your site to read your original content so you have got to be authentic and prove to readers why your content is worth reading. This is when you want to show your personality so that people will read your content and view you as voice of reason in the film world.

Chapter 11: How to Write About Art

Dear Pennies & Pens,

My parents are avid art collectors so they ignited my interest in art from a young age. When I was younger, they were always visiting art shows to purchase original and printed works to decorate our house.

I will admit that I didn't appreciate the art as much growing up. However, now that I am older I see that coming of age in a house surrounded by art dared me to dream and helped me understand that art is supposed to start a conversation.

I remember having many discussions with my parents and telling them which of their new pieces I liked and didn't like. My parents' art collection was my main inspiration for creating "Pen's Eye" the art section on de la Pen...All Pen Everything. I wanted to showcase the work of talented international and multicultural artists as well as connect with artists to start building my own collection.

Pen's Eye features museums and galleries like Dallas Museum of Art, AT&T Performing Arts Center, Houston Museum of African American Culture, The Menil Collection, and the Museum at FIT. Pen's Eye also includes artists like Gray Malin, Derek Fordjour, Marina Romanova-Arnott, Tabitha Brown, That Artista Philece R, Vakseen, Adam Jones, and Nobody.

Discovering new art is a truly exhilarating experience. Art can inspire you, anger you, or make you crazy. This is why writing about art (like everything else) is a process. Once you learn the technique, you will be able to write prolific art posts. Check out my advice below.

1. Do research - When writing about art, you first need to start with research. Research museums, galleries, blogs, and social media. Doing research will help you catch up on the latest news and you will learn more about how the art world works.

You will also figure out where the hottest museums and galleries are. Next, research artists (alive and deceased) to find out who are the top artists and why.

These days, most artists have a website, blog, and social media presence, so be sure to check them out. Additionally, check online galleries that sell and exhibit artists' work. Personally, I am obsessed with this art app called Vango, it is an amazing platform to discover new art.

Lastly, you should research materials and different types of art. This will help you when communicating with other art enthusiasts and artists as well as creating content.

2. Follow artists, galleries, and museums on social media - After discovering various artists, galleries, and museums, you should follow them on social media to keep up with their latest news, events, and projects. This will give you the opportunity to connect with them and start a conversation.

This will also give you a chance to see how artists, museums, and galleries talk about art. This will help you learn the industry lingo which you will need to use in your posts. Using industry jargon will help your peers connect with your work and take your writing seriously.

3. Visit galleries, museums, and artists' studios - The best way to discover great art is to experience it. To do that, you have to put your smartphone and tablet down, and go visit galleries, museums, and artists' studios. Most museums and galleries have days where admission is free or discounted so it's always affordable.

To visit an artist's studio, you do have to know the artist but if you're a blogger, you can visit the artist's website, email them, and ask to come by their studio. Most artists need press coverage so most will be willing to work with you. Especially, if they are not established.

As you visit museums, galleries, and artists' studios, you will experience the art world first hand which will help you develop an eye for art.

4. Attend Events - Museums and galleries are always having events to celebrate new exhibitions or highlight the work of certain artists. Artists will also host their own events in their studio or at other locations to attract media coverage and connect with new clients.

Attending events will help you learn more about art and contemporary artists. You will also have the opportunity to meet and network with artists and other art connoisseurs.

5. Take notes - While doing research online and visiting galleries and museums, you should take notes because you will not be able to remember everything. Write down artists' names as well as the titles of their pieces.

Also, make a list of galleries, museums, and major art events in your city and in other locations. As you do that, write notes to help you remember things about them. Eventually, you will commit this info to memory but when you are starting out, you definitely want to keep track of everything.

6. Start writing - Start writing posts to get the hang of writing about art. Don't worry if your first post is not perfect, your writing will get better with time. Start your post with details like the artist's name, medium of work (painting, sculpting, photography), where the artist is from, etc.

If you are writing about a gallery or museum, give a brief history on the place, then talk about current or future exhibitions. In every post, share your opinion or thoughts. This is how you differentiate yourself from other bloggers.

Do not worry about the fact that you are not an art critic, you will build knowledge and experience in due time. As a lifestyle blogger, you will learn that someone will always be there to tear down your work so do not let the opinions of others dictate what you do.

As far as the writing itself, be creative and let the words flow. You can talk about why you love art, why you chose to write about this event, artist, etc. Every post should its own unique creation; switch up the format so neither you or the reader gets bored.

Chapter 12: How to Write About Books

Dear Pennies & Pens,

Books take you away to a dream world. In my humble opinion, they are the ultimate escape. I have always loved to curl up with a good book. I was also an English major in college and obviously that required a lot of reading so books are second nature to me.

Over the years I have read many books, some were good and some were bad. Although, I would never classify myself as a professional book critic, I do feel like I know what makes a book worth featuring in a blog post. I have written reviews of The King of Style by Michael Bush, Whitney Houston: The Voice, The Music, The Inspiration by Narada Michael Walden, The Teen Vogue Handbook, and Gil-Scott Heron: Pieces of A Man by Marcus Baram.

I have learned that the process to writing a book review is just that...a process. Below, I have outlined my advice on how to tackle writing a book review.

1. **Read the book in a quiet place** - In order to properly review a book, you should first read it in its entirety. Depending on the nature of the book, you may want to read it more than once. I have found that sometimes when you read a book again you catch things that you missed the first time.

Once you get the book, you need to find a quiet place to read it. I know it may difficult with a busy schedule and family, but, try to make this a priority. Reading in a quiet place will allow you to focus on the book and really digest what is happening in it.

2. **Take notes -** As you read the book, take notes. There may be certain things you want to remember to reference in your post.

Write notes character's names, the setting, plot, etc. If it is a non-fiction book, take notes on whom or what the book is about, facts shared in the book, etc.

3. **Do research and learn the details** - Is the book fiction or non-fiction? What is the plot of the book? If the book is a work of fiction, determine if it is romance, horror, sci-fi, etc.

Check out blogs, media outlets, and social media to see what others are saying about the book. You should also do research learn more about the author and publishing company.

Understanding the details of the book will give you background on the book so you know how to approach writing your review.

4. **Analyze your thoughts & feelings** - How did the book make you feel? Why do you think the book made you feel that way? It helps to figure out your thoughts and feelings about the book so you can determine what type of review you will write.

5. **Write your review** - Start your review with all the necessary facts like the book's genre, when it was published, how much it costs, the plot, author bio, etc.

Next, state your opinion of the book. Be sure to talk about what you liked and did not like. It helps to be specific so the reader really gets an insightful review of the book. Overall, your review should be informative, thoughtful, and interesting.

Chapter 13: How to Write Travel Posts

Dear Pennies & Pens,

This past year, I launched a travel series called Pen.Point: The Seasoned Traveler because I wanted to showcase unique travel and hospitality brands. Each brand featured has products or services that can enhance readers' lives.

Pen.Point: The Seasoned Traveler is about inspiring readers to travel by featuring locations that only a "seasoned traveler" would know about. In essence, the series mostly features independent boutique hotels but there are also restaurants, spas, and destinations.

Since launching Pen.Point: The Seasoned Traveler, I have learned how to write travel posts. Creating travel content is not easy but I have come to love it!

I would like to share some of the things I have learned about travel writing with you. Below, I have outlined a list of steps that you can execute to help you write amazing travel posts.

1. Do research - To create travel content, you need to first do research on the hotel, restaurant, spa, or destination you will be featuring.

For hotels, you need to know things like when the hotel was opened, how many rooms it has, what the nightly rates are, where the hotel is located, how many locations it has, and who the hotel is owned by. It is also good to know who the hotel caters to families, couples, groups, etc.

For restaurants, find out what kind of food the restaurant serves, hours of operation, when the restaurant was opened, who the chef is, and who the owner is.

For spas, find out where the spa is, what kind of services the spa provides, and how much the various services cost.

For destinations, visit the city or country's tourism board website. Almost every city in the world has a tourism board with an accompanying website that is designed to help visitors and the media learn more about the destination.

On these sites, you will find info about restaurants, hotels, art galleries, museums, shopping, and activities within the area.

In general, you should also check out other blogs and media outlets to see what they are saying about the hotel, restaurant, spa, or destination. This will give you insight on what the media and the general public thinks of the destination.

2. Take Notes - As you conduct your research, be sure to take notes. You will need this information later once you start writing your post. Make sure you keep all your notes in one central location so you can easily refer back to them.

3. **Create a theme -** To create high quality travel posts, you should create a theme for each post or create a travel series as I have.

Creating a theme helps streamline your content and gives you a focal point. This way, you won't be all over the place with your content. Having a theme makes your life so much easier because it keeps you organized!

To help get your creative juices flowing, let me give you some ideas. Your theme could be wine country in Oregon. The series would then be named "Sipping On The Oregon Trail". This creative title would give readers an idea of what the post is about without revealing too much.

In the post(s), you would recommend hotels, wineries, and vineyards to visit in Oregon's wine country. You can also include tips on how to get around, what to pack, etc. The theme that you choose should be something that you and your readers are interested in and it should fit in with the overall flow of your blog.

4. Find content - Now that you have identified a theme, you need to find hotels, restaurants, spas, or destinations that fit your theme. This is a very important step because it is the content of your post(s).

You want to find places that have similar characteristics but are not carbon copies of one another. This way, each location brings something different to the table but they all fit together like pieces of a puzzle.

5. Find or take high quality photos to use in the post(s) - Once you have decided what location you would like to feature in your post, you need to find high quality photos.

High quality photos are essential to creating a travel post that people will actually read because everyone wants to see what the place looks like before they'll even think about visiting.

To obtain high resolution images, visit the location's website and contact the publicist to request photos. Make sure you let the publicist know that you will credit the photographer. Most locations hire photographers to shoot images so part of their job is ensuring the photographer receives credit for their work. In essence, they will appreciate your thoughtfulness.

Other options include shooting your own photos or hiring a photographer. Please note, these options are only possible when you are in the location you will be featuring or know a photographer who is. If you choose either of these options, check in with the location you will be shooting to make sure they are aware of what you are doing. This is so you have their cooperation and avoid any legal issues.

6. Start writing - One of the most common misconceptions of travel writing is that you have to visit the locations you'll be featuring prior to writing about them. Of course it helps to visit the places you are writing about because you will get firsthand insight and have real life experiences to base your post on.

However, once you master the art of research you will find that you will be able to decipher if a destination is worth featuring based on their website, social media presence, and customer reviews posted on TripAdvisor, Yelp, and OpenTable.

As far as the structure of your post, that is totally up to you. The blank page is your canvas and it is up to you to create your Mona Lisa in the form of a travel post.

To help you get started, you should include details on the location (which you gathered in your research), talk about why you are writing about this location as far as why you like it, why you think your readers will like it, etc.

Make sure you include facts about the location in your post. You want readers to understand that you have done your research and are a knowledgeable resource.

Travel writing is all about telling a story about a specific location. Tell a story with your post, paint a picture. Be as descriptive as possible but also be informative. The reader wants you to provide more information on a place they are thinking of visiting so be the resource they need.

Chapter 14: How to Plan Press Trips

Dear Pennies & Pens,

Before I outline how to plan press trips, I would first like to define what a press trip is. A press trip is when a blogger travels to a particular destination in order to write about the destination.

Press trips are usually a collaboration between the blogger and a sponsor. The sponsor can be a hotel, spa, PR firm, city, etc.
A press trip is a mutually beneficial collaboration because it allows the blogger to travel to a new destination while the sponsor gets promoted via blogs and social media.

A press trip is a business arrangement because both parties are exchanging goods and services. In some cases, a blogger is paid for a press trip. The itinerary for a press trip is planned by either the blogger or the sponsor. If the sponsor plans the trip, then the blogger must abide by their schedule and usually free time is very limited.

Usually in that case, the sponsor has identified a particular blogger they would like to work with and they are doing a special blogger or influencer campaign. If the blogger plans the trip, it is up to them to create their own schedule, pitch to sponsors, write posts and social media content, etc.

Although, it is more work, I personally love planning my own custom press trips. It gives me full control over my schedule, the places I will visit, etc. I can also control who I work with.

In order to have a successful press trip, you should plan your trip so that everything goes off without a hitch. Press trips are already stressful enough because not only are you traveling, you are also there for business purposes so you have multiple items to juggle.

As the old adage goes, "If you fail to plan, you plan to fail." That said, planning will ensure that your trip is successful and yields the results

you want. Creating a schedule will allow you to assess everything that you have planned to make sure you do not pack too many things in one day. You do not want to wear yourself out and not be able to enjoy your trip. With that said, let's dig into how to plan press trips.

1. Make a List of Destinations - Before you can go on any press trips, you have to first decide where you are going. I suggest making a list of destinations you would like to travel to and separating the list based on location as far as local, national, or international.

I recommend tackling local destinations then national and finally international destinations. Completing press trips in this order will allow you to gain experience and learn the tricks of the trade.

2. Create a theme - As outlined in Chapter 13, "How To Write Travel Posts", you should create a theme for your post or travel series. A theme will help streamline your content and give your posts a focal point.

Since you are planning a custom press trip, you definitely want to have a theme so you pitch to brands who fit the theme. The brands that you work with should enhance your theme so keep that in mind when creating your theme.

For press trips, I recommend creating a theme that can be replicated for future projects or a custom theme for that particular trip. A general theme will allow you to go on multiple press trips without having to write new copy, etc.

A custom theme means you have to find a specific angle that focuses on the destination you are traveling to. If you are going to a truly unique destination or if you have landed a major sponsor, a custom trip may be the way to go.

3. Collaborate with brands - Working with brands on a press trip will assist with covering expenses associated with your trip. Brands can offer complimentary or discounted goods and services. In essence, collaborating with brands is crucial to ensuring that your trip is successful.

No matter how large or small a brand is, they are always looking for new marketing opportunities and partnerships. Brands need to reach as many consumers as possible in order to increase revenue and sales.

By partnering with bloggers, brands are granted access to the blogger's audience. Since the blogger is responsible for creating the content, the brands gets all the benefits but none of the responsibilities of the marketing campaign.

Always keep this in mind when pitching to brands because some brands (especially the larger ones) will act like they are doing you a favor by sponsoring you.

In a way that is true but honestly, you will be executing the bulk of the work so really you are the one doing them a favor. Having this in your head will help you maintain confidence and not be intimidated by brands.

As far as identifying brands to collaborate with, you should look to work with brands that align with yours. This means that if you're a 20 something single male blogger, you probably should not pitch to a family vacation resort.

Like most topics covered in this book, collaborating with brands is a process. That said, I will outline how to collaborate with brands for press trips in the next chapter.

4. Plan Your Trip - Now that you have made a list of destinations to visit, created a theme, and identified brands to collaborate with, it is time to start planning your trip. This is a to do list within a to do list so please see the list below.

- **Set a date** - Set a date for your trip. Keep in mind that you have to incorporate the time it will take to travel to and from your

  destination as well as your work schedule, family, budget, etc. All these things will affect when you are able to go on your trip so keep this in mind.

- **Decide how you will travel** - Will you be flying or driving to your destination? It is important to plan this out so you can book your flight or rental car as soon as possible. Your method of travel will affect your trip because every method has its positives and negatives. I would say use your judgment to best assess what method of travel is best.

- **Book your trip** - Now that you know when you are leaving and returning as well as how you are getting to your destination, you can book your trip. Book your flight, rental car, and hotel. Since this is a press trip, some of these items may be sponsored but you still need to make sure everything is confirmed.

- **Create a schedule** - Since your trip is now booked and you have landed sponsors for your trip, you need to create a schedule. List out all the days that you'll be at your destination and plan what you'll be doing and when.

5. Go on your trip - This step should be fairly easy. Lol! Now that you have planned your trip, it is time to leave. Be sure to leave on time and understand that everything will not go the way you plan it. However, everything will work out in the end.

6. Take photos - While on your trip, take as many photos as possible. Take photos on your phone or camera. You want to have plenty of photos for social media as well as for your blog.

I personally do not use my own photos on my blog but that is because I am an awful photographer. Lmao! I do take photos on my iPhone but I only use them for social media.

Taking photos allows you to remember all the places you've visited and they illustrate your trip. Without photos, it's like you were never there. And that is clearly a no no in travel blogging! Take photos of the destination, your sponsor's products or location, and photos of yourself.

7. Take notes during your trip - Since you are visiting a new destination and planning to write about it on your blog, you should take notes. Taking notes will give you points to reference when you are writing your blog post. While on your trip, jot down facts about the destination, your sponsor, the city, country, etc.

You should also make note of how you felt about the trip and certain places you visited. Your personal observations can also be featured in the post.

8. Do live social media updates during your trip - Throughout your trip, you should do live social media updates.

You can do this by sharing your thoughts on your destination, talk about the food you ate, the people you saw, or the events you attended. You can also take photos of your hotel room, car, and trip on your phone and share them on social media.

Live tweeting and instagramming your trip helps keep your audience engaged in your content. Bloggers should use social media to make their followers "feel like they were there". It is about producing unique and original content that people want to interact with.

To create dope content, you have to find moments or things that stand out that will look cool on Instagram or make an interesting tweet. It's about finding an angle and writing the right copy.

For example, when I worked with Omni Dallas, there was art by local Dallas artists throughout the room, I took photos of the pieces and shared via Instagram. I felt like it was a different way of showcasing the room and its exclusive features. Of course I took pictures of the room itself, but the art photos were sick.

You can also refer back to your social media updates when writing your post. Your social media updates can serve as your notebook meaning you can refer back to your posts when writing your blog post.

I recommend that you keep it real on social media. Be open and honest about your trip. Tell your followers what you're doing and why you're doing it. People want to follow bloggers who are authentic, human, and interesting. If you can be all of these things simultaneously, you'll become a dope lifestyle blogger.

9. Start writing - Now that you have completed all of the above, it is finally time to start writing. With travel writing, you want to make your post as personable as possible. Your personal observations are what is going to separate your post from others.

You can talk about what you liked and didn't like about your trip, people you met, places you saw, etc. Be descriptive and use photos to illustrate your words. Be sure to include facts about your sponsor(s) and hype them up as much as possible. Remember without them, your trip may not have been possible so you want them to feel like you really promoted them so they want to work with you again.

You can also include other fun details like things that may have went wrong or you can write about unexpected surprises. The key to making your post truly refreshing is to be original.

Chapter 15: How to Collaborate with Travel & Hospitality Brands

Dear Pennies & Pens,

In the previous chapter, I briefly mentioned how to collaborate with travel and hospitality brands for press trips. Collaborating with brands is a process because it is a business transaction.

You are exchanging goods, services, or money which means there will be negotiations, adjustments, and in some cases contracts. In essence, it helps to learn the process of collaborating with brands so you can execute it properly.

The key to approaching travel and hospitality brands is to write a targeted pitch that shows you have done your research. You want brands to know that you have thought about how you will feature them on your site. You also want them to feel like you understand who they are and will represent them well.

I have worked with a variety of travel and hospitality brands such as The Omni Hotels & Resorts, Lone Star Court, Hotel ICON, Sunset Marquis, The Line Hotel, and V Spa. So let's get to it: How to Collaborate with Travel and Hospitality brands.

1. Do research - When you are approaching a brand, doing research takes a different form. What you want to do here is learn as much as you can about the brand so you can use that knowledge in your pitch.

For hotels, you want to discover the important facts but also find out what the hotel prides itself on. Is it a boutique hotel? Or a luxury hotel? Or maybe the hotel has its own exclusive restaurant?

Knowing these facts helps you stand out in your pitch because the brand feels like you have not only done your research but that you genuinely care. This shows them that you are the right person to represent their brand which is what you would be doing if they say yes to working with you.

2. Find Contact Info - Once you decide what brands you want to work with, you have to find their contact info. Usually, the more important or established a brand is, the harder it is to find the proper contact person. With emerging brands, it can be difficult to find a contact person because the brand may not have a dedicated PR and marketing team.

To find the contact information, check out the brand's website. Once you are on the website, go to the contact page and look for their PR or marketing team's info. Please note the PR and marketing team handles blogger/media relations as well as online marketing for the brand. In essence, they are who you want to connect with to discuss a collaboration.

If you do not see contact info on the "contact us" page, you can also look for a press or media page. The press or media page serves as the brand's online newsroom. In an online newsroom you can find images and press releases as well as media contacts for the brand.

If you do not find contact info on the "contact us" page or the "press" page, then that usually means the brand works with an agency who handles their PR and marketing. You can still find their PR or marketing agency's info via Sir Google, the most powerful search master around.

I usually Google "hotel name pr contact" or "hotel name press release"; from there I narrow it down to find the most recent contact person. For example, if I find a press release, I look for the date it was written/published, and if it's recent (within the last 1-2 years), I contact that person and hope for the best.

If I find a contact person, I verify that they currently work for or with the brand by googling their name along with the brand name. Example: Sue Smith Public Relations Manager at Omni Hotels & Resorts. Usually, this leads me to a LinkedIn, Twitter, or Facebook profile which I can check out and see if the person still works with the brand. If they do, I figure out how to obtain their email address, then contact them.

As you grow as a lifestyle blogger, you will learn that connecting with brand reps is the hardest part of landing collaborations. The key is to be determined to find a point of contact because it is not going to be easy.

3. Write Your Pitch - Please note your pitch is absolutely the most important thing you will send when communicating with a brand. Your pitch is the brand's first impression of you. This means that spelling, grammar, and presentation matters.

Your pitch is going to determine whether or not the brand decides to work with you. If you truly want to work with the brand , you need to spend time writing a quality pitch.

Details of the pitch: Start the pitch by introducing yourself. I state my name and title and include a link to my site. After that, I give a brief description of my site. Next, I talk about the story that I am working on, explaining what it is all about.

When explaining the story you are working on, you want to be creative and make it exciting. You want the brand to feel like you are an innovator and the content that you are going create will to stand out. You also want them to feel like you took the time to plan out the project and you are not just asking for random freebies.

After you introducing yourself and your story idea, talk about why you want to work with the brand and how they fit in with the story. This illustrates to them that you have done your homework and that you know how to represent them.

Lastly, you need to tell the brand what you want from them and the benefits they will receive from working with you. This is essentially your conclusion so make sure it is really strong. Basically, you want the brand to feel like working with you will be an excellent marketing/promotional opportunity for the brand.

4. Sending the Pitch - When you send your pitch is just as important as what it says. I recommend sending pitches Mon-Wed between 8AM-

10AM CST. In general, you can pitch on weekdays during traditional business hours. I specified those days and times because in my experience that is when you get the most responses.

I have found that sending emails after lunchtime is a no no because folks are sluggish after lunch. Also, Thursdays and Fridays are not good either because it is the end of the week. Unless it is urgent or you have previous relationship with the brand, I do not recommend pitching on these days.

5. How to Send the Pitch - As far as sending your pitch, I recommend that you use a scheduling tool called Boomerang for Gmail. Boomerang is amazing!

It is a Gmail app that allows you to schedule emails, receive follow up reminders, and resend emails if you don't get a reply. I absolutely love it and must shout out my business partner Cacha` Lopez for putting me on!

To get it, just google "Boomerang for Gmail" and install the app in your Gmail account. Use Boomerang to schedule your emails and track whether or not your email was opened. Boomerang is free for 10 credits per month. You can also register and pay a monthly fee to use the service.

6. Complete the Media Request Form - Most hotels, PR agencies, and tourism boards create a media visit request form. This form is designed to learn more information about the media outlet seeking to visit the hotel or destination.

The media request form will ask for your name, contact information, website URL, blog stats, social media stats, social media links, and your story angle.

Refer to your media kit to complete the form. Media request forms can be found on the brand's website or they are sent to you once the brand receives your email request. Complete the form and return it to the brand as soon as possible.

7. Write the post(s) - After landing the project, be sure to write and publish at least one post about the brand. Please refer to the previous chapter for info on how to write travel posts.

8. Follow up with the brand - Once you publish the post(s), send links to the brand. Also be sure to promote the post on social media and tag the brand.

In conclusion, landing project with travel and hospitality brands is not easy but it can definitely be done. Follow my tips and you will be just fine.

Chapter 16: How to Create a Media Kit

Dear Pennies & Pens,

In this chapter, I will be talking about how to create a media kit. A media kit consists of information about you and your blog. A media kit should include your bio, your blog's about page, blog and social media stats, as well as a page that lists all the services you offer.

It is used when you are seeking sponsors or advertisers. A media kit is an excellent way to show off your creativity and you can explain what value you offer to a brand.

A quality media kit is informative, organized, and creative. There is no right or wrong way to create a media kit but there are some essential elements that it must have. Below, I am going to outline what pages should be in a media kit.

1. **Cover Page (Page 1)** - This page is extremely important as it is the first thing that people see. The cover page one should be simple but good. My cover page includes my blog's title, a screenshot of my homepage, and my contact info.

2. **Your Bio (Page 2) -** Your bio is about telling the reader more about the person behind the blog. With this page, you want to make yourself look knowledgeable, professional, trustworthy, and creative.

You also want to highlight any major projects that you have done. If you are a new blogger, talk about projects you did prior to blogging. The key to having a great bio page is to make the reader feel like "you have your stuff together" and they should do business with you.

3. **Your Blog's About Page (Page 3)** - Now that you have introduced yourself, it is time to introduce your blog. Tell the reader what your blog is all about, how often you publish posts, when you started it, etc. Be

sure to highlight any major projects you have done or brands that you have collaborated with.

4. **Blog and social media stats (Page 4 and 5) -** On your blog and stats page(s), include how many people visit your blog, how long they stay on the site, and your bounce rate. You can get all this information from Google Analytics.

Also include your reader demographics as far as their ethnicity, income, education level, etc. You can get that info from Quant cast. Lastly, include your social media stats, list out each social network that you are active on and how many people follow you on each one.

5. **Pitch page (Page 6) -** Your last and final page should be your pitch page. This page should outline exactly why a brand should choose to work with you.

For my media kit, I came up with a list of reasons for why a brand would want to collaborate with me. On this page, I sought to address any concerns they may have. I also included a list of the services that I offer. This way they know what they can hire me to do.

My biggest piece of advice for this page is to think like you're a brand manager, publicist, or marketer. That means you have to look at yourself, your blog, and your stats and think about makes you different, and what value you offer to a brand.

With my blog, I focus on creating content for multicultural people. In essence, any brand that chooses to work with de la Pen...All Pen Everything will have access to my multicultural audience.

Not only does that make me stand out from other bloggers, it provides value to a brand because they may be looking for ways to connect with Asian, Hispanic, and African American consumers so what better way to do that than work with me?

In conclusion, your media kit is one of the most important documents you will create for your blog. Your media kit is a promotional tool that helps you land sponsors or advertisers. In essence, it is important to spend time creating a quality media kit.

Chapter 17: How to Write About Brands

Dear Pennies & Pens,

In this chapter, I will be teaching you to write about brands. No matter what type of brand you are working with, if you are collaborating with them then you are representing them.

That said you want to be able to put your best foot forward. If you can show brands that you are professional, knowledgeable, and creative you will land more projects in the future.

As I stated previously, brands are a business and they exist to make money. That said, when brands work with bloggers it is essentially a content marketing partnership. The blogger creates content that speaks highly of a brand's products or services in exchange for complimentary products, services, or financial sponsorship.

As a lifestyle blogger, you have to learn the process of creating content about brands because you must please the brand as well as your readers. The brand wants you to promote them but at the same time you must be honest with your readers and remain authentic.

You cannot just gush over a brand because they are sponsoring you. Tell your followers the truth because honesty is the best policy. Also, I recommend that you like the brands you work with, this way you do not have to worry about faking it.

It is hard to create content about brands because the content must be creative, high quality, and interesting so that your followers want to engage with it. If you don't like the brand, it will make creating content that much harder because it's not genuine.

Lastly, you must note that your readers and followers look to you for advice, recommendations, and entertainment. They see you as a resource, someone they can trust. The relationship you have with your readers and followers is one that you want to protect at all costs because without it you have nothing.

Your readers and followers engage with your content so they are the reason you are landing brand collaborations in the first place. Having said all that, let's start talking about how to write about brands.

1. Do research - Start your research by visiting the brand's website. This will give you more information on the brand as well as the products or services they sell. The brand's website will also give you insight on the voice and tone of the brand.

The voice and tone of a brand is basically how the brand talks about and presents themselves. Is the copy on their website more upbeat and funny or is it casual and cool? A brand writes their website and marketing copy to appeal to their target consumer. Understanding this will give you insight on who the brand is seeking to reach.

You want to understand the voice and tone of a brand so that you can imitate it in your blog posts. Additionally, check out the brand's social media accounts. This will give you insight on how the brand markets themselves to consumers and how they interact with their followers.

Lastly, you should check out other media outlets and blogs to see what they are saying about the brand. This could give you additional information about the brand and help you understand how your colleagues feel about the brand. Once your research is complete, it is time to start writing your posts.

2. Start with the facts - When you write your post, start with the facts. Include things like where the brand is located, hours of operation, what products or services they sell, when they were founded, etc. Starting with the facts is a great way to introduce the brand to your readers.

3. Get creative - Next you want to get creative in the post. Talk about why you like the brand, as well as their products or services. Include

84

details on why you decided to write about this brand and how their products or services have benefitted you.

Your creativity shows your readers that you genuinely like the brand and you are not writing about a brand because you got complimentary products, services, or financial sponsorship.

4. Take or use high quality photos - Pictures are worth a thousand words. It is so important to use high quality photos for posts about brands.

You do not want to land a collaboration with a brand only to use grainy photos that make the brand look bad. Remember, the purpose of your post is to make the brand look good.

I recommend obtaining photos from the brand, taking your own photos, or hiring a photographer. How you execute this is up to you just note you have to use amazing photos that illustrate the text of your post.

5. Link to the brand's website and social media in the post - Always link to a brand's website and social media in the post. This way your readers can connect with the brand online or purchase something.

6. End the post with a bang - Be sure to write an amazing conclusion to the post. You can reiterate your points about why you like the brand and their products or services.

The key to this step is to leave the reader wanting more in the aspect that they cannot wait to see what brand you will write about next. You also want the reader to follow the brand online or purchase from the brand...an excellent conclusion will guarantee this.

Chapter 18: How to Attend and Cover Events

Dear Pennies & Pens,

I love attending and covering events because you get to meet new people, experience new products, sample delicious food, sip on drinks, and so much more. I think lifestyle bloggers should attend as many events as possible. It presents the opportunity to network and discover new things to feature on your blog and social media.

I have attended events such as New York Fashion Week, Charleston Fashion Week, Artopia in Dallas and Houston, Affordable Art Fair NYC, Fashion X Dallas, Dallas International Film Festival, Untapped Festival, New Cities Summit, Style.uz Art Week, and the M&TVA Awards.

There are two types of events that you can attend and cover press previews and general public events. Press previews are for bloggers, journalists, editors, writers, and photographers only. Press events are produced by brands or their PR/Marketing team. Media events are about introducing a new product, location, or service to the media.

General public events are open to anyone who purchases tickets or RSVPs for the event. Since these events tend to be larger and more well-known, the media is usually required to secure a press pass or media credential in order to attend.

A press pass serves as a ticket to the event for members of the media. A press pass allows the media to attend the event for free or pay a media rate. The media rate is always less than what regular attendees pay.

Now that I have broken down the different types of events, I am going to outline the process of attending and covering events. Check out the list below to see how to attend and cover events.

1. Find events to Attend - Search Google, social media, and websites like Eventbrite or Meetup to learn about upcoming events.

Look for events that seem interesting and fit in with the aesthetic of your blog. Keep in mind that certain events are annual and only take place once a year, other events will be special events that only happen once, and some events happen more often such as once a month. The brand or PR agency organizing the event usually determines how often it takes place.

There are many different kinds of events you can attend as a lifestyle blogger. You can attend fashion shows, art exhibitions, wine tastings, music festivals, panel discussions, conferences, seminars, meetups, networking events, sporting events, awards shows, etc. The options are endless, you just have to find them.

2. Visit the event website - Now that you have discovered events you would like to attend, go to the event's website to obtain more information. You need to know what time the event starts and ends, where it will take place, and purpose of the event.

Conducting research helps you learn more about the event so you can start thinking about the type of post you will write. Research will also help you determine if the event is worth attending and you'll be able to gauge how popular the event is.

3. **Visit the media page on the event website** - Upon visiting the event website, look for a media or press page. This page will list the Publicist or PR Agency's contact info. Once you have their email address, email them and ask for a press pass to cover the event.

In some cases (especially with large or popular events), this page will have a media credential application. A media credential application is created by the brand or PR agency hosting the event. The purpose of a media credential application is to learn more about the media outlet interested in covering the event.

The standard media credential application asks for your name, website URL, social media handles, blog stats, and what type of coverage you are planning to do. After you submit the application, it is then reviewed by the brand or PR agency hosting the event.

Once they receive the application, it is either approved or disapproved. Common reasons for the application not being approved are the outlet does not reach many people or the application was incomplete.

When completing the media credential application or asking for a press pass, be honest and keep it real. You should mention major projects that you have done, events you have covered, and brands you have worked with. You want the brand or PR agency to know that you are a serious blogger who is going to get the job done.

4. Attend the event - Now that you have obtained a press pass, you need to make sure you actually attend the event. This may seem obvious but you would be surprised at how many bloggers say they want to cover an event and then don't show up at the last minute.

I will admit, I am guilty of doing this but it is a very rare occurrence. Not attending events you are scheduled to cover makes you look unprofessional. Always attend events you are committed to cover.

5. Utilize social media during the event - While at the event, whip out your iPhone or Android and take pictures of the people, the food, the clothes, the drinks, the art, yourself, and other things. Snap plenty of photos at the event and upload them to Instagram or Twitter during the event.

Be sure to tag the brand or PR agency hosting the event in your posts so they can like or comment on the photo. Same thing with Twitter and other social networks, tag the brand in posts so they can RT your tweets.

The key to live tweeting is to talk about what's happening at the event. Tell your followers who's there by name dropping celebrities, influencers, bloggers, and media outlets. You can also explain what the event is all about; disclose the location of the event, etc. Live tweeting is all about making everyone who's not at the event feel like they were there.

During events, I mostly use Twitter and Instagram. I also use Swarm (previously Foursquare) to check-in to the event's location. This is an easy way to tell the world what event you are attending and why. Also, you can share Swarm check-ins on Twitter and Facebook so it's a one stop shop.

6. Take notes during the event - I will admit I have an excellent memory so I rarely take notes during an event. However, I do recommend that you do take notes on what you liked or didn't like about the event, who was there, etc. Your notes will help with writing your post on the event.

7. Write your review of the event - Unlike other posts, event reviews should follow a standard format. Start the post off with the name, date, and location of the event. Then outline the event's purpose or concept.

Next, you should include details on whether or not it was a media event or if was for the general public. It is important do this because it lets your readers know whether or not they would be able to attend the event in the future.

After you do that, tell your readers what you liked and didn't like about the event. This makes your post more personal and helps the reader to visualize what happened at the event.

Personally, I adopt positive/negative writing. If I have negative things to say, I say something positive first. For example: I loved the decor but the food wasn't my favorite.

You do not want to offend anyone or burn bridges by writing negative things. However, you have to keep it real and be authentic for your readers or else they will stop reading. Writing event reviews is like walking on a tightrope but you will get the hang of it.

8. **Email your post to the brand or PR team** - After publishing your post, email it to the brand or PR agency who hosted the event. This is great a way to build relationships and get invited to future events.

Overall, covering events is interesting, fun, hard work. You get to meet new people, taste new food and drinks, see amazing clothes and art, and hear amazing music. It is well worth it!

Chapter 19: How to Conduct Interviews

Dear Pennies & Pens,

In this chapter, I will be talking about how to conduct interviews. As it states on Wikipedia, "An **interview** is a conversation between two or more people where **questions** are asked by the interviewer to elicit facts or statements from the interviewee."

Interviews help you and your readers learn more about what your interviewee does, their creative process, and their background. Interviews are also excellent networking opportunities because it gives you the opportunity to make new connections. Additionally, interviews drive traffic to your site because your interviewee will usually promote the post on their social networks.

I have interviewed a variety of artists and entrepreneurs such as Kelly Cutrone, Andre Leon Talley, Gene Noble, Marina Romanova-Arnott, Derek Fordjour, Adam Jones, and Tabitha Brown. Conducting interviews is more than asking a few questions. It takes hours, days, weeks, and sometimes months to coordinate, execute, and publish interviews.

To properly conduct an interview, there are a few steps that you should complete to ensure the final post is the best that it can be. Check out the list below.

1. Decide who you would like to interview and why - Do you want to interview your favorite designer, author, producer, publicist, editor, or stylist? Why? Did you love their latest collection, book, movie, or editorial? Or maybe they have a new project that you'd like to find out more about?

Having a specific reason for why you would like to interview someone will help you when setting up the interview and compiling a list of questions.

2. Do your research - Everyone has a website and/or blog, so visit your prospective interviewee's website or blog, and take notes. Read their about page to get their full biography, and then check out their press page to see what publications have featured them.

Next google your interviewee's name and see what other blogs and websites have said about them. It is important to know what your media colleagues are saying about your prospective interviewee because it will help you determine how the media and the public feels about them.

3. Contact the interviewee or their Publicist - Reach out to your prospective interviewee or their Publicist to see if they are interested in working with you. I believe this should be done prior to writing interview questions because if the subject is not interested, you can save yourself some time.

Depending on who you are seeking to interview will determine if the person sets their own schedule or if they have a Publicist that represents them.

It should be noted that a Publicist is responsible for coordinating media interviews for their client. A publicist has full access to their client's schedule and they know it better than their client so they are definitely who you want to contact.

The good news is a Publicist is looking for bloggers who want to interview their client, so you would be making their job easier. In the email, you should introduce yourself and your blog. Tell them who you are, what your blog is all about, and why you would like to do the interview.

This same rule applies if you contact your interviewee directly; they will still need to know more about you and your site before they agree to the interview.

The only suggestion I have for contacting an interviewee directly is to set a deadline for the project. The interviewee is probably managing

multiple projects so letting them know what your deadline is will help them plan their schedule.

4. Decide if the interview will happen in person, via phone, or email

In person interviews are great because you can make eye contact with the subject and truly get a feel for their personality. These details could be included in the final article thereby making it more unique. However, with an in person interview you'll need a camera to shoot a video of the interview or to take photos of the interviewee.

Unless you are a videographer, photographer, or know someone who is, an in person interview can be more difficult to coordinate and execute. This is because the video interview will have to be edited as would photos meaning it will take longer to publish your final post. Nonetheless, in person interviews are still awesome because you make a real connection with the subject.

Phone interviews are the next best option to in person interviews. The phone interview allows you to connect with your subject and get the information you are looking for. Not to mention, both you and your interviewee can be in your respective locations during the interview.

With phone interviews, make sure you either record the interview to be transcribed later or take notes. It is important to record your interviewee's responses properly so you don't misquote them. You should also clarify to make sure your notes make sense.

Email interviews are the absolute easiest. The great thing about email interviews is you simply write the questions and email them to the interviewee to be answered. The great thing about email interviews is that you do not have to worry about misquoting the interviewee or the responses not sounding like something they would say.

Overall, my advice is you evaluate each method and decide which works best. Think about your work schedule, personal life, etc. and decide what makes sense for you and your interviewee and take it from there.

5. Write Interview Questions - Use your research and notes to compile a list of questions. Only ask about 5-10 questions, this way you get good information but do not overwhelm the interviewee by asking for their life story. It also helps to ask specific questions about their work or life, especially if the interviewee is already well known.

I always ask about their background like how they started their career or business, what they are currently working on, and their plans for the future. Sometimes, I also ask a fun question like "If you could live anywhere in the world, where would it be and why?" This lightens the mood and makes the interview more interesting.

When writing your interview questions, think about what you would like to know about the interviewee or what makes them special. Then create 5-10 questions around that.

It is best to start with their background finding out where they grew up and went to school, and then ask about how they started their business, etc.

6. Publish the final post - Publish the final post with the interview in its entirety. If it is a video interview, simply embed the video on your blog. However, you should introduce the video with a few written sentences and then let the video speak for itself.

If the interview was done via phone or email, include the full text of the interview in question and answer format, as well as photos of the interviewee and their work.

7. Send the interviewee a link to the post - The final step is to send the interviewee a link to the post.

If you connected with the interviewee via their Publicist send the link to the Publicist and they will forward it to their client. It is important to let the interviewee and/or their team know you completed the project so they will want to work with you again.

Chapter 20: How to Build Your Network

Dear Pennies & Pens,

In this chapter, I will be talking about How to Build Your Network. Let me start by saying that I love networking! I mean my agency is called The Network, lol!

But seriously, networking is crucial to growing your blog and business. After all, "it's not what you know but who you know." Networking is essential in the blogging and social media industries because you will receive support to launch creative projects.

However, most people do not know how to build their network. Building your network is so much more than attending events and handing out business cards. There is a true art to networking. Check out the list below to learn How to Build Your Network.

1. Create a list - Create a list of brands, bloggers, publicists, marketers, entrepreneurs, and industry peers that you want to meet. Identifying a list of people you would like to meet or work with will help you come up with an action plan on how to contact them.

2. Connect online & then reach out - Follow your favorite brands, bloggers, and industry insiders online on social media. Following people you want to connect with helps you stay up to date on their latest news or projects. This way you can learn more about the person or brand and develop a relationship with them.

To score brownie points and get on their good side, be sure to RT them, comment on their blog, and share their content on other social networks.

After you follow the person or brand online, reach out to them and say something nice. Do not just follow them and expect them to notice you.

When you reach out, be real and authentic, but also be a bit of a kiss ass. No really, if you want someone to notice you (especially if they are more established), you must compliment them first. It is a guaranteed way to get on their good side.

After the initial interaction, ask if you can connect via email to chat more. Then once you score their email address, shoot them a quick email reminding them of how you met. Connecting with the person via email allows you to establish an offline connection and begin building a solid business relationship.

3. Attend events - Attend events to connect with people in person. My advice is that you go to different types of events so you meet all kinds of people. When you attend events, I recommend that you go alone because it will force you to network and meet new people.

While at an event, put your phone down, walk around and mingle. Strike up conversations with people by complimenting them or asking them what they think of the event. It will take time to learn how to break out of your shell and network with people but you will get there in due time.

Be sure to bring business cards to the event but only give out business cards to people that you have had a conversation with. Please do not be that random person who walks around handing out business cards for no particular reason. It will be much more genuine and real (not to mention more cost effective) if you only give cards to people that you have met.

4. Talk to family & friends - When it comes to networking, you should definitely talk to family and friends. You would be surprised to find that your husband's sister's BFF is the Head of Marketing at Brand X.

We often forget that our family and friends have careers and businesses since we usually do not discuss business with them BUT we have to remind ourselves that they do. This means they could be connecting us with people to network with. Do not overlook this very untapped into resource!

Talk to family and friends about your blog and business. Tell them about the projects you are working on and ask if they know anyone who does something similar, etc.

5. Scope social media - Scoping social media is about looking for new contacts that you do not know. This one is a little tricky but if done right can work wonders. What you want to here is let it happen organically.

While on social media, keep an eye out for cool and interesting people who have similar interests as you. When you discover new people; visit their website or blog to learn more about them. After that, reach out to the person. I have found some of many business contacts by connecting with like-minded people to build an offline relationship.

6. Connect via email - Once you start building a rolodex of new contacts, start connecting with them via email. In the initial email, you should introduce yourself then tell the person more about your blog. Be sure to highlight major projects you have completed and tell them what you are currently working on.

7. Meet in person - Now that you have new business contacts, you want to meet them in person. Meeting in person helps solidify the relationship and "put a face with the name."

The internet and social media has made it easy to avoid people in real life but it is imperative to building a long lasting business relationship. Meet with new business associates for lunch, drinks (happy hour), or coffee.

During the meeting, be nice, courteous, and relaxed. People want to work with people who are nice and chill. Keep it professional during the meeting but you should also let your human side show.

Crack jokes and tell a few personal anecdotes. Do not tell them your life story but do allow them to see that you are a real person...it makes you more relatable and down to earth.

It will take time to build a solid network but if you work on it regularly, you will get there. These tips are designed to help you explore new ways of building a rolodex of business contacts.

Chapter 21: Marketing Your Blog

Dear Pennies & Pens,

Most of this book has focused on teaching you how to create content and collaborate with brands. However, this chapter is about teaching you how to market your blog.

It is great to spend time creating dope content but if no one reads it, you've wasted your time. Below, I have outlined how you can promote your blog.

1. **Create business cards** - Create business cards with your name, your blog's name, website URL, and your social media handles. With a business card, you can promote your blog while running errands, attending events, etc.

2. **Link to your blog in your email signature and on social media** - Create a link to your blog in your email signature. This way everyone you email will have a link to your blog.

Also include your blog link in all your social media profiles. This way anytime you get new followers or someone checks out your page, they can check out your blog.

3. **Talk about your blog to everyone as much as possible** - The more you talk about your blog, as far as telling people about your triumphs, tribulations, and upcoming collaborations, the more people will take interest in what you are doing.

Friends and family will support you and frenemies will note that they need to step their game up. You do not want annoy anyone but you need people to see how much you care about your blog so they will feel the same way.

4. Attend Events - Attend blogging conferences, social media seminars, product launches, art exhibit openings, fashion shows, concerts, and more to meet people, network, and promote your blog.

It is cool to connect with people online but there is nothing like making a face to face connection. As a lifestyle blogger, you want to attend a variety of events so you build a diverse rolodex of contacts.

5. Create a social media marketing strategy - Social media is the main place where you should promote your blog because you can link to your posts directly thereby driving traffic to your site. That said you should create a social media marketing strategy for your blog.

You need to outline your goals, objectives, and tactics within your plan. Be clear about what you would like to achieve and also be realistic about the time and energy you can devote to social media marketing.

6. Use social media - Now that you have created an official marketing strategy it is time to use social media to actually promote your blog.

I recommend focusing your efforts on 1-2 social networks although you should develop a presence on the big three: Twitter, Facebook, and Instagram. Honorable mention goes to Pinterest, Tumblr, YouTube, Google+, and Swarm (Foursquare). I only recommend using 1-2 primarily because you are only one person and you do not want to spread yourself too thin.

Although brands like it when you are active everywhere, it is more time effective to focus on 1-2 social networks. Unless you are a major brand with a full team, you will find yourself neglecting social media altogether because you will be so overwhelmed. To decide which social networks to focus on, simply consider which ones you like best and which ones are best fit for your brand.

I personally like Twitter and Instagram the most; Twitter is a great place for me to share my thoughts, opinions, and latest projects. Instagram allows me to communicate my brand in a visual way by sharing photos from my blog, events I am attending, projects I have done, etc.

Be sure to use social media as much as possible. In the world of social media, you are only as a relevant as your last post so be sure to produce content and update as much as possible. Share your content multiple times a day since people are on social media at different times.

Additionally, you should view everything as a content opportunity. If you are at an event, check in on Swarm (Foursquare), tweet about who's there, or a post a selfie to Instagram. By doing this, you've updated your social networks as well as effectively promoted the event, and your blog.

7. Email Marketing - Email marketing is still an effective way to market your blog. With an email newsletter, you can send your latest posts to readers, business associates, brands, friends, and family.

The best part of an email newsletter is that it comes to the person's email inbox so as long as they open it; it is more likely that they will read and engage with your content.

I use Mailchimp for my email newsletter. Mailchimp has an RSS feed feature that you can connect to your blog's RSS feed and Mailchimp will automatically email subscribers your latest posts. I love this feature because it means I don't have to create a newsletter every time I publish a post.

8. Phone calls & text messages - I know this sounds kind of old school but it works. These days, people are always plugged into their phones so it is a great way to market to them directly. Also making phone calls or sending text messages makes people feel special because you have gone out of your way to let them know what you are working on.

Please note that this tactic works best amongst friends and family but you should only do this when you land major collaborations or if you're hosting a giveaway. This way you are not harassing people that you are close to.

9. Comment on blogs - This is another old school tactic but it still works especially if you do it properly. Check out other blogs and look for posts that are similar to yours or are about topics that you know a lot about.

Write a comment and find an authentic way to mention your blog. I would like to emphasize being authentic so you don't upset the other blogger by promoting your own content.

Here's an example: if I read a post about how to collaborate with a hotel, I would write the following comment "This was such an insightful post! I have also collaborated with hotels to write reviews for my blog. I wish I would have known some of these tips then!" -- Notice the comment is related to the original post but it also promotes my blog in an authentic way.

Someone could read this comment and think I would like to check out LoudPen's hotel reviews then take action to visit my blog. In essence, I have promoted my blog but not upset the other blogger by spamming their blog with an unrelated comment.

10. Write for other blogs - Writing for other blogs is a fantastic way to promote your blog. It gives you access to that blog's readers and the opportunity to position yourself as an expert. It is also a great way to hone your writing skills because you have to learn how to write for a new audience.

In order for this to be an effective promotional tool you should find a blog that is more established than yours or at least on the same level as you. If you want to promote your blog, you need to reach a larger audience so you have to work with an established blog.

Chapter 22: How to Measure Your Blog's Success

Dear Pennies & Pens,

There are many ways to evaluate your blog's success and reach. It is important to be able to measure your blog's success because it will help you when pitching projects to brands.

In my opinion there are levels of influence and a variety of ways in which a blogger's influence can be measured. I believe this because every blog is different as is every blogger. Some bloggers are the equivalent of a small business since they only reach a small or local audience whereas other bloggers are like major brands because they reach millions of people all over the world.

I believe that every blogger (no matter how large or small) deserves a place in the blogosphere. However, I have noticed that because numbers are the easiest way to measure influence that is all people focus on. Numbers can change at the drop of a hat so bloggers should explore other methods for measuring their influence.

As a blogger, if you are able to measure your success in a variety of different ways, it will show companies that you understand your value and worth. More importantly, it will give you the confidence you need to seek out collaborations with brands. Below is a list of ways that will help you track the success of your blog.

1. **Being invited to unsolicited events -** When brands invite you to events that you did not request an invitation or media credential to attend, it means they believe that you are an influential blogger.

By inviting you to an event, companies are asking you to come experience their product or service so you can write about it on your blog. In essence, they want you there because they believe that consumers listen to you and you are the right person to spread the news of their latest products and services.

104

2. **Receiving free products** - When a company agrees to send you free products to review on your blog, you are now successful.

It costs money to make and ship products so if a company finds you worthy of a free product, then they like your blog and believe that you are the right person to promote their company. This is very important and proves that your blog has become successful.

3. **Receiving unsolicited press releases** - When you receive unsolicited press releases, the PR agency or brand feels that you are an influential blogger and they want you to share their latest news with your followers.

4. **Constantly receiving new followers, likes, or comments** - When your Twitter, Instagram, Facebook, etc. are all blowing up with notifications of new followers, likes, or comments, you are doing your thing! Gaining new followers means that people are seeking to connect with you and they like what you have to say.

Receiving likes and comments means that people are engaging with your content. In essence, if you receive these notifications consistently, then you are posting content that causes people take action. People are inundated with social media content so if they interact with yours it means the content stands out.

5. **People actually read your blog** - Once your blog starts being read by at least 5-10 thousand people per month, you are successful. Although, you will not be considered the most successful blog, it will be clear that you have developed an audience.

6. **When you pitch to brands and they respond** - When you pitch to brands and they respond to your email (even if it is to say no), you have built a successful brand.

If a brand rep takes time out of their day to respond to your inquiry or pitch, it means they considered your pitch and checked out your blog.

Brands receive pitches for sponsorship all the time and they cannot respond to each one. In essence, if a brand responds to you, then your blog and pitch stood out so much that they felt compelled to reply.

7. **When people ask about your blog** - If someone asks about your blog, you are doing something right.
People have so much on their mind these days with technology, family, and work so if they remember that you have a blog and take time to ask about it, it's because they care. Congrats, you are now successful.

8. **When major brands engage with your content** - When your favorite brand likes one of your photos, Retweets you, or better yet, if they respond to you on social media, you are definitely a successful blogger.

Some brands receive hundreds if not thousands of social media mentions per day. In essence, if they take time to respond to you or engage with your content, they like what you are doing or saying.

9. **When you start to ruffle feathers** - When you start to ruffle feathers, you know you are successful.

This will happen when someone writes a negative comment on your blog, or says something rude to you on social media. Instead of getting upset, think of it this way, your writing affected someone so much that they felt the need to attack you on social media.

Sometimes your biggest haters are your biggest fans who are really just jealous trolls. Take it with a grain of salt and keep it moving.

10. **When you land press mentions** - When other blogs and media outlets start mentioning your blog, you are now successful. People view you as an authority and think that your blog is worthy of being checked out.

11. When you have monetized your blog – Once you have successfully monetized your blog, you are truly successful. At this point, you are working with brands to create sponsored posts, have advertisers, and

you do speaking engagements. Many bloggers who reach this level also end up launching other businesses to make more money.

In conclusion, each of these methods will help you in determining the success of your blog. As I said, I think it will help you to focus on some of these items instead of measuring your success solely on numbers. Numbers will make you crazy and worst of all, you will never have enough!

Chapter 23: Productivity Tools to Help Manage Your Blog

Dear Pennies & Pens,

Throughout this book, I have talked about how to create unique and original content for your lifestyle blog as well as how to work with brands. Since this is the last and final chapter, I would like to give you a list of tools that you can use to help you manage your blog.

Each of these tools will help you manage your blog and social media presence. Each tool on this list is one that I have personally used and can vouch for. Check out the list below.

1. **Basecamp** - Basecamp is a project management tool. You can use Basecamp to create projects and within a project you can create and manage to do lists, add files from MS Office or Google Docs, create text files, add images, assign tasks to team members, etc.

Basecamp has truly been a lifesaver for me! Best of all you can try it for free for 60 days, and if you upgrade the plans are super affordable.

2. **Evernote** - Evernote is absolutely amazing for note taking, brainstorming sessions, and saving content you find while surfing the web. Remember all the previous chapters that included doing research and taking notes as part of the process of creating blog posts? Evernote is where you can take notes and store them in one place!

In Evernote, you can create notebooks (a collection of notes) and organize those notebooks based on topic, project, etc. How you organize your Evernote is up to you.

My favorite part of Evernote is the Web Clipper feature. It is an extension in Google Chrome and it is amazing! Once you install the extension, you can save articles, images, text, into Evernote to read or view later.

Evernote and Evernote Web Clipper are free to use. Evernote does have paid subscription options but if you are not ballin out of control, the free version will work just fine.

3. **MailChimp** - I have been using MailChimp for some time now and I love it! MailChimp is a tool that allows you to create and send email newsletters. I use it to send out de la Pen's newsletter as well as sending press releases for The Network. Mailchimp is awesome because it's so easy to use and customize. It's also free for email lists of 2,000 or less.

The best part about MailChimp for bloggers is you can automatically send out newsletters using your blog's RSS Feed. Once you set it up in MailChimp, every time you publish a new post your newsletter goes out. You can also track your analytics as far as knowing who opened your email, if they clicked any of the links, etc.

4. **Buffer** - Buffer is a social media management tool. It allows you to create posts for Twitter, Facebook, LinkedIn, and Google+ to be scheduled to post at certain times. In essence, instead of logging into each social network, you can login to Buffer and post to all your channels from there.

My only issue with Buffer is that they only offer a 7 day free trial and after that you have to upgrade to a paid plan. But other than that, Buffer is super clean and has one of the easiest to use interfaces out there. It is definitely a tool that will help with marketing and promoting your blog.

5. **Hootsuite** - Hootsuite is also a social media management tool. Hootsuite is the truth.com for those with little to no budget. You can schedule posts for Twitter, Facebook, etc for FREE! It's pretty awesome.

Hootsuite also offers paid subscriptions that offer more options. Hootsuite also has an app available for iPhone and Android so you can schedule posts on the go. It's pretty dope.

6. **Google Apps for Work** - This is a tool that allows you to use Gmail and all its features but with your own domain name. In essence, your

email would be yourname@yourdomainname.com and your email looks and works just like the traditional Gmail.

With Google Apps, you have Gmail, Google Drive, Hangouts, Google Calendar, Google+, and more. It is a one stop shop! You do have to pay for Google Apps but it is well worth it! I highly recommend this amazing tool.

7. **Google Drive** - Google Drive is a tool that comes with a Gmail account (both free Gmail accounts and paid Google Apps accounts) that allows you to create and store files (images and documents) online.

Google Drive can be accessed from any device which means you never have to look for anything, email something to yourself, or worry about losing anything.

8. **Gmail** - A Gmail account gives you Google Drive, Google+, Google Calendar, etc. all for free! I do recommend that you create a professional email so that even though you are using the free version of Gmail, you still look professional. If I had Gmail, I would go with LoudPen@gmail.com or something to that effect.

9. **Boomerang for Gmail** - Boomerang is a Gmail app that allows you to schedule emails, receive follow up reminders, and resend emails if you do not get a reply.

If you have a full time job, a family, etc you are going to need this to schedule emails because you are not always going to have the same schedule but your email must go out at a certain time. Boomerang is free to use for 10 emails per month; if you need or want more than that, you will have to buy a subscription.

10. **Google Chrome** - This is a web browser made by Google. I love Google Chrome; it is easy to use and super-fast. When you are blogging, tweeting, and conducting research, you need a browser that fast and reliable. Google Chrome is the best one!

11. **Google Analytics** - This is a tool made by Google that allows you to track your blog and website statistics. With Google Analytics, you can see how many visits your blog gets per day, week, month, and year. You can also see where your readers are located and if they visited your site after a Google search or if they came from social media.

It is an awesome tool that you definitely need. As a Lifestyle Blogger, you have to be able to show brands that you have built an audience and you understand how to measure success. So having a Google Analytics account and regularly checking your stats is a must.

The stats you see in Google Analytics will also help with creating future posts because since you know what posts were the most popular, you can duplicate posts like that. Google Analytics is free so there's no reason for you not to have an account.

12. **Bluehost** - Bluehost provides domain names and hosting services for websites and blogs. I absolutely love Bluehost. They are the only hosting provider or domain registrar, I would recommend.

If you purchase hosting and your domain name from Bluehost, everything will be in one place. In essence, you will only have to login to Bluehost to renew your hosting or buy a domain. Bluehost also has really awesome support, they are helpful and they don't try to sell you random crap you do not need. Bluehost also allows you to set up your site with WordPress, Weebly, and much more. I swear by Bluehost, they are just that dope!

13. **WordPress** - WordPress is a Content Management System (CMS). It allows you to create and manage a website or blog. There are two versions of WordPress: WordPress.org and WordPress.com.

To use WordPress.com, all you have to do is visit the website, create an account, and then create your blog. It's completely free to use. The only thing you would have to pay for is your domain name.

However, WordPress.com is limited, you cannot sell ad space and it doesn't have all the functionalities of WordPress.org. But if your cash is low or you just started blogging and are not ready to make a financial investment in blogging, it is a great option.

WordPress.org is considered to be the professional version of WordPress. That's because WordPress.org requires a monetary commitment since you have to purchase hosting and a domain name.

WordPress.org's software is free to download but again you have to buy a domain name and hosting in order to make your site live on the internet. WordPress.org is awesome because you have more options for blog templates and you can use plugins. "**WordPress plugins** are bits of software that can be uploaded to extend and expand the functionality of your **WordPress** site." (WordPress)

I use plugins like Disqus Comment System and HS Social Media Buttons. The Disqus plugin allows me to use the Disqus comment system to manage blog comments. The HS Social Media Buttons adds buttons that link my social media accounts so that people may follow me on social media after visiting my blog.

I recommend WordPress.org for professional bloggers or bloggers who want to be professional bloggers, there's so much you can do with it! Plus even though you have to pay for certain items, it's worth investment.

14. Swarm - This one may seem random since it's a social network but Swarm is an amazing tool for productivity! Swarm is an app that allows you to check in to locations and share with other social networks like Twitter and Facebook. Swarm was created by Foursquare (the original app that did what Swarm does) to make a better experience for users.

I love Swarm because when I go to events, restaurants, hotels, etc., I can check in to the location and it will be stored into my Swarm account. When you attend as many events as I do, it's impossible to remember the name of each one. So when I go to events, I make sure I check in on Swarm so it'll save the location for me to reference later.

This is extremely helpful when writing blog posts about events, restaurants, hotels, etc. For example, when I wrote a post on restaurants in Dallas, I could not remember the names of the restaurants but the food was so good, I knew I had to feature them on the site. So I went into Swarm, scrolled through my check-ins and voila all the names were there.

15. Password Keeper - Password Keeper is an app that allows you to save all your passwords. With all these tools I have recommended, you're going to need Password Keeper because who can remember all those usernames and passwords?

Password Keeper is free to use and it offers the option of buying a backup plan so you can back up your passwords.

16. Songza - Songza is a free music streaming app that recommends playlists based on the time of day, your mood, or activity. It may seem odd that I included this as a productivity tool but I truly believe that it is.

Music can help motivate you when writing a blog post or thinking of ideas for a brand pitch. Songza has so many playlists that you'll never get tired of it. I wrote this book while listening to Songza, it is just that awesome.

In Songza, you can favorite playlists and share songs or playlists via Twitter and Facebook. So not only does Songza give you motivation music, it also gives you social media content.

17. **Echofon** - Echofon is a Twitter app. It is my favorite Twitter app because it is easy to use and you never miss notifications of new followers, favorites, @ replies, DMs, etc.

18. **Social Media** - As a blogger, you must have every major social network's app downloaded on your phone for instant access. You should have Facebook and Facebook Pages Manager, Tumblr, Twitter, Instagram, Pinterest, Google+, LinkedIn, and YouTube.

19. **SquareFX** - This is app is for resizing photos so that they fit into Instagram. It is pretty awesome; I use it all the time!

20. **Photoshop Mix** - This app allows you to edit photos, combine two images to make one photo, and so much more! It's fabulous and I appreciate my business partner for putting me onto this one.

21. **Cal by Any. Do** - Cal helps you plan your day. As a lifestyle blogger, you'll be juggling multiple projects so being able to keep track of everything is a must. Use Cal to create a daily, weekly, or monthly schedule for yourself.

Cal also syncs to Google Calendar so you'll have it multiple places. Cal also sends reminders to let you know what tasks or events you have coming up.

22. **Dropbox** - Dropbox allows you to store your photos online and you can share the photos with others for them to view and/or download. Dropbox can be accessed online from a PC or on your phone through the app.

Once you start doing photo shoots or collecting photos to use for blog posts, you'll find that the images are taking up massive space on your hard drive. To avoid this, store all your photos in Dropbox.

This concludes the list of productivity tools that will help with managing your blog. Hopefully, this list has given you some new apps and tools to download that will increase your productivity.

Chapter 24: Conclusion

When I started writing this book, I had no idea what it was about. I just knew I was writing a book on blogging. I was back in my hometown of Cincinnati enjoying a much needed break and spending time with my family when I had a convo with BFF and decided to get serious about writing a book.

I figured that writing a book on blogging would make the most sense because so many people have asked me for advice on how to become a blogger, where to find content, etc. So when I got back to Texas, I wrote a list of chapter titles and just started writing.

I didn't create an outline for the book; I just let it develop itself. That said it wasn't until later that I truly understood what this book was about and what its true value is. I know that sounds totally backwards but that's the way my mind works. Lol!

I wrote this book because I want to help people and make money; plain and simple. As far as the process, writing #MakeUrPenLOUD was truly the hardest thing I have ever done. I started writing the manuscript in September and I finished it in January. Upon completing the manuscript, I assumed that the book was done. I knew I needed to edit the book but I had no idea it would take as long as it did.

Writing the book was easy because I have been writing for years. However, it was the editing process that I had a daily love/hate relationship with. Some chapters were easy to edit because it was just a matter of rearranging words to make the content flow better. Other chapters required a full rewrite.

Since I plan to publish other books in the future, I decided that my editing process should consist of three phases: the 1st edit, the 2nd edit, and the 3rd edit. The first edit would be me reading the manuscript chapter by chapter and editing the writing only.

The second edit would consist of editing for spelling, grammar, structure, and flow. The third and final edit would be about ensuring the book is consistent and does not overuse certain words/phrases, has no typos, spelling, or grammar errors.

The editing process took about 3 months. I am the ultimate perfectionist so while editing I would often agonize over the smallest details. Is there a better way to say that? Am I explaining this correctly? Would this make sense to someone else?

Since this is essentially a how to book, creating it was not just about writing, it was about helping people learn a new skill. This book is the first product that I have created with the intention to sell; therefore, I wanted to make sure that the book delivered on its promise. The last thing I want is for people to purchase this book and want their money back.

As a creative entrepreneur, my pockets seem to have more lint than money which means anything I buy has to be worth the money. I figured that my readers would be in the same boat so I wanted to make their purchase one they would not regret. Additionally, I truly want to help people.

I wanted to write a book that would become a "classic". Something that people would read and reference for years. I want to use this book to create a platform to host a series of events about lifestyle blogging and social media.

My main goal with the events is to help people but also to be accessible. I want any and everyone who desires to attend my events or buy my products to be able so. I do not want people to have to struggle, get a second job, or take a second mortgage out on their house to purchase what I am selling.

To wrap this up, I would love to tell you what my favorite chapters of this book are. When I wrote the outline for this conclusion, I was definitely going to. However, each chapter is my favorite because this

book is my favorite. To me #MakeUrPenLOUD is the best book ever because it was written by me, lol!

As far as my future plans, I am going to focus on The InkSpot and 8515. I fully intend to build an empire and my ultimate goal is to be able to walk into any fashion show, beauty product launch, art exhibition, hotel, restaurant, or event and people say "Omg, that's LoudPen!"

This book is just the beginning; the start of something great. This book is about making you feel inspired, empowered, and motivated so you can learn to be the best lifestyle blogger that you can be.

Before my pen runs out of ink, I would like to tell you who my "Pennies and Pens" are. That would be you, my dear. I saved the best for last because Vanessa did.

And there it is: #MakeUrPenLOUD: How To Be A Lifestyle Blogger.

About LoudPen

LoudPen is a Lifestyle Blogger, Editor, Publicist, Stylist, CEO of The InkSpot, Co-Founder of 8515, and Author of #MakeUrPenLOUD: How To Be A Lifestyle Blogger. Over the past 7 years, LoudPen has gained extensive experience in lifestyle blogging, writing, editing, marketing, social media, public relations, creative direction, styling, brand management, and event production.

LoudPen has worked with brands such as Omni Hotels & Resorts, Rimmel London, and Macy's. LoudPen has established herself as an influencer on social media with thousands of followers on social media. As a lifestyle blogger, LoudPen has learned how to create and market content as well as how to collaborate with brands and cover events. Most importantly, LoudPen has mastered the art of creating and building a successful online brand.

A few months ago, LoudPen decided to share her knowledge of lifestyle blogging and social media with the world by writing #MakeUrPenLOUD: How To Be A Lifestyle Blogger. LoudPen wants to inspire and empower readers by helping them learn how to create unique and original content.

LoudPen is also Co-Founder of 8515 - a multicultural lifestyle agency. We specialize in multicultural and millennial marketing. 8515 offers marketing, public relations, event production, branding, management, creative direction, styling, writing, editing, blogging, and social media. 8515 works with fashion, beauty, music, art, travel, and lifestyle brands.

Last but not least, LoudPen is CEO of The InkSpot. As CEO of The InkSpot, LoudPen oversees the development and execution of all projects. LoudPen created The InkSpot in order to build a global empire like Jay Z and Oprah. LoudPen is currently based in Dallas, Texas since relocating from NYC in November 2013.

Thank You

I would like to thank my parents, siblings, aunts, uncles, cousins, friends, and my business partner for always supporting me. I love you and appreciate everything you have done for me.

- LoudPen

www.ingramcontent.com/pod-product-compliance
Lightning Source LLC
Chambersburg PA
CBHW060945040426
42445CB00011B/1009